# VEGETARIAN MICROWAVE COOKING FOR ONE & TWO

## CAROL BOWEN

Grub Street • London

First published in 1996 by
Grub Street
The Basement
10 Chivalry Road
London
SW11 1HT

Copyright © Grub Street 1996
Text copyright © Carol Bowen 1996

Photographs by
Sian Irvine

Illustrations by
Juliet Dallas-Conte

**British Library Cataloguing
in Publication Data**

Bowen, Carol
Vegetarian Microwave
Cooking for 1 and 2
I. Title
641.5636
ISBN 1 898697 31 0

Designed by
Adam Denchfield Design

Printed and bound in Italy by
Vallardi Industrie Grafiche Sp A

For Peter, who has gradually become
accustomed to a meal without meat.
His amusing comments, wry sense of
humour and amazing ability to taste dishes
at a moment's notice have been invaluable.
His seemingly insatiable demands for meal
variety and generous man-sized portions
means this book is likely to please the
most ardent former meat-eater and
committed vegetarian alike.

# Foreword

The marriage between the microwave and the vegetarian or non-meat eater is a fine one. Not only because the microwave makes light work of cooking many of the vegetarian's 'staple' foods like vegetables, rice, pulses, grains, fruit, nuts and cereals but because it cooks them to perfection. Gone are the days of limp greens, soggy over-cooked pasta, over-sticky rice and nutritionally-poor fruit, for such foods emerge from the microwave fresh, colourful, flavoursome, nutritionally-rich and moreover, most appetising. Even if some of the time-savings are minimal on some foods, such basics do cook with the minimum of attention and can be left until just cooked to the right stage be it tender-crisp, 'al dente', fork-tender, softened, melted or caramelised.

This book is about cooking small amounts of food for vegetarians or meat-eaters who wish to eat 'vegetarian-style' with the minimum amount of fuss. It's for people who perhaps have little time to spare and appreciate the speed a microwave offers in cooking a multitude of dishes; vegetarian couples who don't want to be a slave to the kitchen, especially after a long day at work; those who are cooking an extra vegetarian meal for a member of the family or a friend, whether it be a staggered family meal-time or special dinner party; and also those living or dining alone who have adopted a vegetarian lifestyle whether they are a student in a bed-sit, elderly person cooking at home or family member at 'home alone' for the night.

Such like-minded individuals can relax safe and secure in the knowledge that their healthy lifestyle is enhanced by using the microwave to prepare nutritious meals. Coupled with all the other benefits a vegetarian diet promotes, from less heart disease and intestinal disorders to a more ecologically sound way of life, the microwave and the vegetarian are an unbeatable team on all fronts!

The food market has responded handsomely to the trend towards vegetarianism and microwave manufacturers have kept pace with developments to assist the vegetarian too. Our supermarkets are groaning with fresh fruit and vegetables, many of them organic in origin; dairy products have developed apace with new vegetarian cheeses, low-fat yogurts, fromage frais and bean curds introduced to the chilled cabinet on a regular basis; and whole aisles (not just a measly single shelf) are now devoted to wholegrains, pulses, rices, flours, pasta and soya derivatives; and chilled displays of ready-prepared salads, be they savoury or sweet, are temptingly prepared fresh on demand from which the family, duo or single diner can choose everyday. The choice and variety of foods offered to the vegetarian has never been greater nor more easily accessible. Supermarkets also have electronic tills which means that you can buy as much or as little as you want so there is no need for unnecessary wastage or forced meal repetition.

Microwave manufacturers have responded by producing a range of models that suits the lifestyle and the pocket of virtually everyone - be they the adventurous family cook, no-frills student diner, newly-married couple who share the cooking; or elderly person watching the food and fuel bill. Microwaves are now available from the low-cost, minimum-space, no-extras or basic 'budget model' to the sophisticated high-tech, multi-function, 'all singing and dancing' luxury oven, and there are countless variations between the two extremes.

If there is an underlying general theme to all the different types of vegetarian who are cooking in small portions in their vastly different models of microwave then it is perhaps that none of them want to spend too long preparing their meals. I have tried to keep this common trait in mind while developing and selecting the recipes for this book. I realise that there are times when even beans on toast seems a chore to cook and that at other times you want to push the boat out because you are entertaining, have a little more time to spare, or are simply bored stiff with ready-meals, the take-away or your more usual repertoire of meals.

You will therefore find recipes suitable for a lazy brunch on a Sunday, a mid-week speedy supper, lunch for a two-some, packed work-day meal ideas to ring the changes to the sandwich trolley, meals to impress when you want to entertain, and a few ideas that you can shop for on the way home and still have time for yourself after preparing. Some are traditional while others are in line with today's lighter, healthier trend towards food; some inspired by regional cuisines the world over; some devastatingly simple while others are more challenging; and there are recipes to fit every pocket from the pauper to the prince. The basic know-how section at the beginning of the book should also give the low-down on microwave cooking if you're a microwave novice or new owner, or give a refresher course to those who are more familiar.

I hope that you will enjoy my selection, find that some become long-standing favourites and finally be rewarded with good, long health.

CAROL BOWEN

# At a glance contents

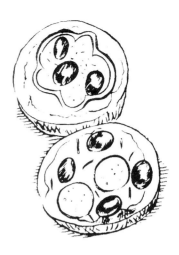

**SWEET ENDINGS**

# Introduction

## WHAT ARE MICROWAVES?

For centuries people have cooked food to make it more palatable, easier to digest and moreover safe for consumption. From the early days of the cave man's smoky fire through to today's high-tech microwave ovens, the principle of heating food to cook it has remained the same; the difference is in the speed of cooking and the methods employed. Traditional methods of cooking food in the fire, in the gas or electric oven and under or over the charcoal grill use conduction as the prime method of introducing heat to food to cook it. But what do microwaves do, what are they and where do they come from?

The mechanics of microwave cooking are surprisingly simple and certainly no more magical than a television or radio. Inside the microwave is a magnetron vacuum tube - this is the 'heart or brains' of the microwave and converts ordinary household electrical energy into high-frequency electro-magnetic waves, called microwaves. Once produced, the microwaves are then directed into the oven cavity, through a wave guide and stirred,

by a fan, for even distribution.

The waves are then either reflected, pass through or are absorbed by different materials. Metals reflect them (so cooking utensils must be non-metallic); glass, pottery, china, paper and most plastics allow them to pass through (so they make the most ideal cooking utensils) and foods absorb them.

The microwaves are absorbed by the moisture in food, causing the food molecules to vibrate rapidly, thus producing heat to cook food. Imagine the boy scout rubbing two twigs together to light a fire and you have the general idea. However, the speed at which the microwaves cause the molecules to vibrate is millions of times per second - thus producing a remarkably intense heat that cooks extra fast!

It is a completely different method of cooking food compared with conventional methods (where heat is passed along a chain from one molecule to the next until the whole becomes hot and cooked) - especially since dishes remain cool, metals cannot be used and timings are extra speedy... and as a result different cooking procedures and techniques are called into play.

## THE MICROWAVE COOKER

All basic models are pretty much the same in design. They consist of a cabinet, magnetron, wave guide, wave stirrer, power supply, power cord and controls. Some have special extra features like automatic defrost, variable power control,

turntable, integral thermometer or temperature probe, browning or crisping elements and stay hot devices. Varying only slightly in design, they all work in the same way - microwaves are produced in the magnetron and are passed into the oven cavity through the wave guide to be stirred by a fan. Once there, the microwaves are safely contained in the cavity since the base and the walls are made of metal and deflect the microwaves into the food. All cooker doors and frames are fitted with special seals as an extra safety measure to ensure microwaves stay in the cooker. In addition, all microwave cookers have one or more cut-out devices so that the flow of microwaves stops automatically whenever the door is opened or indeed if the door has not been shut properly.

Within the vast selection of microwave ovens available three basic models can be identified:

### Portable Microwave Ovens

These are undoubtedly the most popular ovens on the market. Almost as light and certainly as portable as a TV they simply require a 13 or 15 amp plug for use and will happily sit on a convenient work surface, trolley or other firm, stable surface for operation.

### Double Oven Cooker

A few microwave models are available teamed up, and in the same unit as a conventional cooker - here the microwave acts as a second or double oven. Most models are built-in but a few are available free standing.

## Combination Cookers

This is an expanding section of the market and one that is likely to attract second-time buyers. These cookers have the facility to cook by both microwave and conventional means in one single operation and in one unit - they can also operate in tandem or sequence with each other or separately, as liked. Some models offer further choices with fan-assistance, grilling and automatic roasting controls linked with the microwave.

## INSTALLATION

All that is required to install a portable microwave oven is a fused power socket, making such cooking machines popular choices for students, flat-dwellers, the elderly as well as families with staggered meal times.

Manufacturers also recommend that you place the microwave on a stable surface and have adequate ventilation. It is therefore possible to site the microwave in a multitude of places. Mine sometimes sits on the work surface and more often finds itself on the trolley so that I can wheel it around from room to room and even out to the terrace for outdoor eating - giving useful flexibility of cooking.

If you plan to build-in your microwave to kitchen units then ensure that you buy the correct fixing kit or housing unit. Make sure there is adequate venting, and always check your microwave handbook for any special instructions.

## OVEN CLEANING

Here is another bonus! Since the walls to the oven cavity of the microwave remain cool during cooking, cleaning is often just a quick wipe operation. Food does not have the opportunity to bake-on. Simply wipe, at regular intervals or as spills occur, with a damp soapy cloth - after disconnecting the oven from the electrical supply. Remove and wash oven trays, shelving and bases if possible in the same way, or according to the manufacturer's instructions.

Wipe over the outside surfaces and the door of the oven regularly but do not allow water to seep into the vents. If possible, also clean any air filters or stirrer fan guard according to the instructions in your handbook.

Stale cooking smells can be removed by boiling a solution of 3 parts water to 1 part lemon juice in a bowl in the microwave for about 5 minutes on HIGH, then wipe with a cloth to dry.

Also remember to have your microwave checked by a qualified engineer every 12 months, or as recommended by the manufacturer.

Do not operate the oven when it is empty. For safety, especially when young inquisitive hands are around, place a cup of water in the cooker when it is not in use. If the cooker is accidentally switched on the water will absorb the energy - then there is negligible risk of damaging the magnetron.

## FACTORS WHICH AFFECT MICROWAVE COOKING

### Starting Temperature of Food

Foods which are cooked from room temperature will take less time than foods that are frozen or chilled. Cooking times in the recipes that follow refer to a starting temperature of foods as they are normally stored, unless otherwise stated.

### Density of Food

The denser the food, the longer it takes to cook. Heavy, dense foods like potatoes will take longer to cook than light porous foods like sponge cakes. For the same reason a solid, dense mass of food like a whole cauliflower will take longer to cook than the same when it is divided and cut into small florets and spread out for cooking.

### Composition of Food

Foods which are high in fats and sugars will cook faster than foods high in liquid because fats and sugars absorb microwave energy more readily. They also reach higher temperatures during the cooking process than water-based foods. It therefore takes more time to cook foods which are high in moisture like vegetables, than it does to cook those with little moisture like cakes and breads.

### Quantity of Food

As the volume or quantity of food being cooked in the microwave increases, the cooking time increases. If you double the amount of food, the time will increase by about one-half as much again.

## Size and Shape of Food

Smaller pieces of food will cook more quickly than larger pieces, and uniformly shaped pieces cook more evenly than irregularly shaped ones. With unevenly shaped pieces, the thinner parts will cook faster than the thicker areas and should be placed towards the centre of the dish where they receive less energy. Ideally, portions of food that are of the same size and shape cook most evenly. It is also important to remember that round and ring shapes cook more evenly than square, oval or rectangular shapes. With the latter the energy seems to concentrate in the corners and can cause charring - to overcome this, protect the corners with small pieces of foil to shield them from the energy.

## Height in the Oven

Areas that are closest to any source of energy cook faster than those further away and the microwave is no exception to this rule. Depending upon its design your microwave may cook faster near the floor or the roof where the energy source is located. Rotating, turning over and stirring of foods will minimise this effect.

## TECHNIQUES

As with any new appliance, and certainly one that has an unfamiliar cooking action, there are a few simple techniques to ensure cooking success:

## Stirring

Stirring is an operation that is carried out when cooking conventionally and is also applied when cooking by microwave. Conventionally we stir from the bottom of the pan to the top to distribute the heat but with a microwave this is from the outside to the centre of a dish for even cooking. Precise stirring instructions will be given in a recipe if it is important, if not a simple stir halfway through the cooking time will usually suffice.

## Rotating

If your model of microwave has a turntable then this cooking technique becomes redundant. If it hasn't then a simple quarter or half-turn of the dish at regular intervals during the cooking time will ensure even cooking when a dish cannot be stirred or turned over.

## Turning Over

Many large dense items of food like potatoes often appreciate

turning over after about half of the microwave cooking time to ensure good results.

## Arranging

The careful arranging of foods in a dish for microwave cooking can mean the difference between a perfectly cooked ingredient and an adequately cooked one. For success follow the guidelines below:

• try to cook foods of an even or similar size together and if possible arrange in a ring pattern leaving the centre empty.

• if foods are of an irregular shape, like spears of broccoli, then arrange the thicker sections to the outside of the dish where they will receive the most energy to cook.

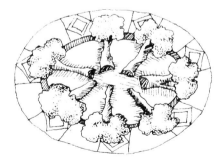

• for plated meals that need reheating, ensure the food is spread evenly across the plate or that thicker pieces of vegetables are to the outer edge where they receive most energy.

• wherever possible ensure that the depth of the food in a dish is even - if not, stir or re-arrange to compensate for this.

## Re-arranging

Re-arranging foods cooked in the microwave will also ensure evenly-cooked results - even if your microwave has a turntable. Once during the cooking time is usually sufficient - moving foods from the outside of the dish to the centre and vice versa.

## Shielding

As with conventional cooking some parts of foods are more vulnerable to over-cooking than others. The ends of vegetable and nut roasts, the ends of stuffed marrows and courgettes are examples. In such cases it is considered acceptable to introduce

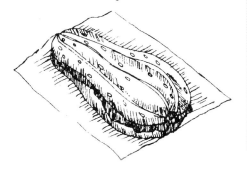

small strips of aluminium foil to protect such areas (although do check in your microwave handbook for specific advice).

This is the only time when metal may be introduced into a typical microwave oven and it is important to make sure that it does not touch the oven walls. Position on the food for half of the normal cooking time and secure with wooden cocktail sticks if necessary.

## Covering and Wrapping

Drying out, spattering of walls and slower cooking times than needed can all be eliminated by covering or wrapping foods for the microwave. Covering will 'lock-in' and contain juices and speed up cooking times by trapping heat-retaining steam.

There are several ways to cover or wrap foods for cooking:

• use a tight-fitting purpose-made lid or improvise with a saucer or plate for the same effect.

• use double-strength plastic cook bags especially for vegetables but replace the metal ties with rubber bands, string or plastic clips.

• cover with a tight membrane of microwave-safe plastic cling-type film but puncture the top or turn

back a vent to prevent a 'ballooning' effect. Take care however when removing since it will trap steam which burns.

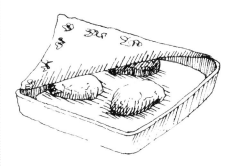

• use absorbent kitchen paper as a base to stand food on or as a cover for the same. It is especially good for absorbing excess moisture in foods that appreciate crisping like the skins of jacket baked potatoes and the crust of bread. It is also invaluable for drying herbs and when dampened for reheating and steaming pancakes and similar products.

## Observing Standing Times

Food still continues to cook by conduction when microwave energy has been turned off. This is not a special action devoted to the microwave alone - the same action happens to a lesser degree with conventional cooking and it must be catered or allowed for. For this reason it is important to err on the side of safety and undercook rather than overcook food to allow for this action. Additional cooking time can always be added after observing the standing time if the dish is still inadequately cooked but there is no rescue package for an overcooked one.

### Removing Excess Cooking Juices

Any juices that seep from a food will continue to attract microwave energy (especially vegetables with a high water content) - if these juices are considerable and the cooking time is longer than say 5 minutes on HIGH, then it is advisable to remove them with a bulb baster regularly during cooking so that they do not prolong the cooking time appreciably. The juices can always be re-introduced towards the end of the cooking time if the dish starts to dry too much.

### Releasing Pressure in Foods

Foods with tight skins or membranes like vegetarian 'sausages', jacket potatoes, apples and egg yolks must be lightly pricked prior to cooking or they are liable to burst or explode. For the same reason boil-in-the-bag pouches and microwave cling film must be cut or vented to prevent a ballooning effect - this is because of the tremendous amount of pressure that develops within such quickly cooked food.

### Browning Foods

As a result of little applied surface heat over short cooking times - foods cooked in the microwave do not readily brown. To encourage and assist or disguise the browning process try one of the following tips if you like:

• grill foods like gratins before or after microwave cooking.

• use a special microwave browning dish especially for foods like fried eggs, toasted sandwiches and stir-fries.

• buy or make your own browning mix to coat foods -paprika, toasted breadcrumbs, crushed crisps, soy sauce, Worcestershire sauce and soup mixes are good ideas that work well.

• baked items like cakes, biscuits, breads and muffins could be coated with toasted coconut, chocolate vermicelli, chopped nuts, chopped glacé fruits, poppy seeds, herbs and many dark coloured spices like cinnamon or ground mixed spice.

• ice or frost a cake or baked item after cooking.

## A FEW RESTRICTIONS

The following foods do not cook well in the microwave:

### Eggs in Shells

These are liable to explode due to the build-up of pressure within the shell.

### Popcorn

This can prove to be too dry to attract microwave energy although some manufacturers have produced microwave popcorn - popcorn in a special bag with seasonings and flavourings that works superbly.

### Batter Recipes

Items like Yorkshire puddings, soufflés, pancakes and crêpes need conventional cooking to become crisp and firm. The microwave will however make the basic sauce for a soufflé and reheat pancakes and crêpes very efficiently.

### Conventional Meringues

These should be cooked in the conventional oven since they do not crisp and dry sufficiently in the microwave.

### Deep-Fat Frying

This is not recommended since it requires prolonged heating, it is difficult to control the temperature of the fat and the food may burn.

### Liquids in Bottles

Check that bottles do not have too narrow necks or built-up pressure may cause them to shatter.

## DISHES AND UTENSILS

Without doubt, the range of cooking utensils that can be used in the microwave oven is wider than those used for cooking conventionally.
A few exceptions do, however, exist:

## Metals

Most manufacturers object to the use of metal. Even small amounts in the oven will reflect the microwaves so that they do not penetrate the food to be cooked. Therefore, avoid metal dishes, baking trays and metal baking tins, foil dishes, cast-iron cookware, plates and china trimmed with a metallic design, metal kebab skewers, any dish with a metal screw or attachment and the paper coated metal ties often found with freezer and cook bags.

## Glass, Pottery and China

Ovenproof and plain glass, pottery and china are all suitable. Be sure to check that they do not have any metallic trim, screws or handles, and, if using a pottery dish, that it is non-porous.

## Paper

For low heat and short cooking times, such as thawing, reheating or very short prime cooking, and for foods with a low fat, sugar or water content, paper is a good utensil. Napkins, kitchen paper, cups, cartons, paper freeze wrap and the paper pulp board often used for supermarket packaging are all suitable. (Kitchen paper or paper towels are specially useful for cooking fatty foods, since they absorb excess fats and oils and can be used to prevent splattering on the walls of the oven).

Wax-coated paper cups and plates should be avoided since the high temperature of the food will cause the wax to melt; they can, however, be used for defrosting cold items like frozen cakes and desserts.

## Plastics

'Dish-washer safe' is a useful indication as to whether or not a plastic is suitable for microwave use. Plastic dishes and containers, unless made of a thermoplastic material, should not be used for cooking foods with a high fat or sugar content, since the heat of the food may cause the plastic to melt and lose its shape. Plastic film for microwave use and devices like boil-in-the-bags work well. Pierce the bag or film before cooking to allow steam to escape, and take care when removing the plastic film in case any steam remains. Do not attempt to cook in thin plastic bags as they will not withstand the heat of the food. Thicker storage bags are acceptable. Use elastic bands, string or non-metal ties to secure the bags loosely before cooking. Melamine is not recommended for microwave cooking since it absorbs enough microwave energy to cause charring.

## Cotton and Linen

Napkins are ideal for short warming or reheating procedures like reheating bread rolls for serving. It is important only to use cotton or linen containing no synthetic fibres.

## Wooden Bowls and Bakeware

These are only suitable for short reheating purposes, otherwise the wood or wicker will tend to char, dry out or crack.

## Roasting Bags

A very clean, convenient way of cooking many foods. This is particularly true of nut and vegetable 'roasts' since browning takes place more readily in them than other plastic bags. However, the plastic ties must be replaced with elastic bands or string. Snip a couple of holes in the bag to aid the escape of steam.

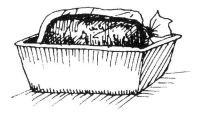

## Microwave Containers

With the increased popularity of microwave cooking comes a host of special innovations in microwave cookware. Several ranges manufactured from polythene, polystyrene and thermoplastics are now widely available and come in a comprehensive range of shapes and sizes.

## Thermometers

Ones made specially for microwave ovens are available but can be used in an oven only when specified by that oven's manufacturer. Since their main use is for checking the internal temperature of a meat roast they have very little use for the vegetarian microwave cook. They can be used however to check that the internal temperature of ready-made meals is sufficiently high enough to kill off all food organisms after cooking for the recommended time. Some newer ovens have an automatic cooking control, a temperature sensing probe, that can be inserted into the food while in the oven. When the food reaches a precise temperature, the oven turns itself off automatically.

### Browning Dishes

Available from most microwave dealers and large kitchenware stores, these duplicate the conventional browning and searing processes of conventional cooking. Especially useful for pre-browning vegetarian burgers and vegetarian sausages, they can also be used for 'frying' eggs and sandwiches, and browning vegetables. The browning dish, made of a glass ceramic substance with a special coating that absorbs microwave energy, is preheated in the microwave until the base coating changes colour, usually about 8 minutes on HIGH (follow specific manufacturer's instructions). The food is then placed on the dish to brown and turned to sear the remaining sides. Preheating times and browning or searing times differ according to the food being cooked and the power output of the oven. Always follow the manufacturer's instructions.

### Remember

If you are going to cook food in both the microwave and the conventional oven, be sure to use an ovenproof dish. Here's a simple

test to check microwave suitability:

Fill a heatproof glass cup with water and place in the utensil being checked. Place the utensil in the microwave oven and cook for 1¼ minutes. If the water is warm in the cup and the utensil is cool, go ahead and use the utensil. If the utensil is warm or oven hot and the water is still cool, or barely lukewarm, do not use it for microwave cooking.

### The Shape of Dish to Use

After checking the material of the dish or utensil, consider its shape, too. Ideally, the more regular the shape the better it is suited to microwave cooking, e.g. a round shape is better than an oval. A straight-sided container is better than a curved one, as the microwaves can penetrate more evenly. A large shallow dish is better than a small deep one as the food offers a greater surface area to the microwaves.

### DEFROSTING

During the early introductory years of the domestic microwave it was frequently referred to as 'the unfreezer' since one of the major advantages and bonuses of owning a microwave was its ability to defrost food quickly and efficiently.

Capitalising on this effect, almost all microwave manufacturers have introduced a special DEFROST control or button to ensure good defrosting microwave action. This control programmes the microwave to introduce just the right amount of energy to defrost food without cooking it - it does so by turning the power on and then off at regular intervals over a period of time.

It is possible to simulate this action by turning a microwave without such a control manually on and off at regular intervals with rest periods in between but it is rarely as successful and can be time-consuming.

### Defrosting Tips

• Defrost food slowly - never try to hurry the process or there is a danger of cooking the food or drying it out unnecessarily.

• Frozen foods wrapped in freezer foil or foil containers should be stripped of their covering and placed in a suitable dish for the microwave.

• Separate vegetarian sausage links, blocks of foods and stacked items like vegetarian burgers and layered pancakes as they defrost.

• As with cooking, prick, slash or vent membranes like microwave cling film before defrosting.

• Turn foods over, stir or rearrange to ensure even defrosting at least once during the expected defrosting time.

• Remove excess drip or thaw juices with a bulb baster during defrosting if they become excessive.

• Remove metal lids and open cartons before defrosting.

• Crisp items like breads, cakes and biscuits will appreciate sitting on absorbent kitchen paper during defrosting.

• If you intend to defrost and cook in one operation straight from the freezer then follow all the guidelines on stirring, turning, rotating and re-arranging foods, not forgetting to allow a standing time too.

## REHEATING

Most foods will reheat successfully in the microwave cooker without loss of quality, flavour, colour and some nutrients. For best results follow the guidelines below:

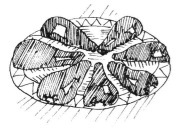

• Arrange foods on a plate for reheating so that the thicker and denser portions are to the outer edge where they will receive most energy.

• Cover foods when reheating with a layer of microwave cling film if there is no lid to retain moisture.

• When reheating, observe the standing time action to make maximum use of the microwave energy and to prevent overcooking.

• When reheating potatoes in their jackets, breads, pastry items and other moist foods, place them on a sheet of absorbent kitchen paper so that it will absorb the excess moisture.

• Stir foods regularly while reheating. If stirring is not possible, then rotate the food or dish or re-arrange it.

## COOKING SEQUENCE OF MEALS

As a general rule for microwave cooking, cook the main course first. Most main course dishes, especially those in sauces, do improve upon standing and vegetarian roasts will usually be easier to carve after standing too.

Obviously, cook foods that require a long standing time first. Last-minute or quick-cooking dishes can be cooked during that standing time.

For ease of preparation and cooking, prepare starters and desserts well ahead and reheat if necessary just before serving. A pudding that needs little attention can often be cooked while you are eating the starter and main course.

Menu planning and serving food that is perfectly cooked is an art that comes with practise and experience. Your microwave cooker will help you through this trial and error time if you err on the side of safety. Dishes that have become lukewarm will quickly reheat with perfect freshness rather than having a dried-out look. Certainly until you have got the measure of your microwave do not attempt to reheat, thaw or even cook more than one dish in the oven at the same time - it is easy to over-estimate the time required and forget the composition of the dish so that foods cook unevenly.

## ADAPTING RECIPES AND SCALING DOWN TO SERVE 1 & 2

Many of your favourite family recipes can be converted for use in the microwave simply by adjusting, and often shortening, the recipe cooking time. The ideal way to start to convert a recipe is to study the recipe carefully and check whether there are any familiar techniques in its method such as steaming, roasting or poaching that you can easily convert. Check that all the ingredients included can be cooked in the microwave and refer to procedures and times from other standard microwave recipes to work out your cooking times.

The following checklist will help you with the conversion, but use it only as a guideline - rely upon your own judgement for best results:

• In general terms, foods cooked in the microwave take about one-quarter to one-third of the time they take when cooking conventionally. But do however, allow for standing times. The exceptions are boiling rice and pasta which still require almost the same time as conventionally since this time is required for the rehydration process. Once cooked however, rice and pasta can be reheated far more quickly in the microwave than conventionally.

• Check the cooking process regularly. Stir and rearrange foods if they appear to be cooking unevenly.

• Use less liquids when cooking items like casseroles and soups and in cooking vegetables.

• Foods tend to rise higher during microwave cooking so, in general, choose large containers.

• Reduce flavourings like herbs and spices by about one-third since the flavours of these seem to be intensified during microwave cooking.

• Wherever possible, cut food into small, even-sized pieces so that they are small and uniform in shape for quick cooking.
Many microwave recipes produced by manufacturers are geared to serving a family of 4 or more - but don't despair and discard your handbook, for such recipes can usually be halved or quartered to serve 1 or 2.

### As a general guideline:

• If you wish to make a recipe that serves 4 serve only 2 then halve the amount of each ingredient given and microwave for about two-thirds of the given cooking time.

• If you wish to make a recipe that serves 4 serve only 1 then quarter the amount of each ingredient given and microwave for about one-third of the given cooking time.

• Always err on the side of safety by undercooking rather than overcooking, especially with delicate egg or cream-based dishes.

• Choose smaller cooking dishes but stir, turn and rotate just as frequently.

• Leave to stand for 3-5 minutes after cooking to observe standing times rather than the usual 5-10 minutes usually recommended for large portions of food.

### GUIDE TO THE RECIPES

All the recipes that follow have been tried, tested and developed for serving 1 or 2 people.

All the recipes in this book were created and tested using microwave ovens with a maximum power output of 650-700 watts. The ovens also had variable power and the descriptions used refer to the following power outputs:
**High = 650-700 watts or 100%**
**Medium = 375-400 watts or 60%**
**Defrost = 225-250 watts or 40%**
**Low = 175-200 watts or 30%**

The chart on page 17 gives the approximate power input in watts at these levels and their relative cooking times.

The microwave ovens used for testing also had a turntable facility - if yours does not then follow the rules on turning, rotating and rearranging in the introductory chapter.

NB: Metric measurements may vary from one recipe to another within the book and it is essential to follow **either** metric or Imperial. The recipes have been carefully balanced to get the very best results using only one set of measures and cannot be interchanged.

**Note that unless otherwise stated:**
• flour is of the plain variety

• eggs are size 3

• all spoon quantities are measured level

| GUIDE TO COMPARATIVE MICROWAVE OVEN CONTROL SETTINGS | | | | | | | | | | | | | |
|---|---|---|---|---|---|---|---|---|---|---|---|---|---|
| Settings used in these recipes | Settings variations on popular microwave ovens | Approximate % power input | Approximate power output in watts | Cooking times (*in Minutes*) (for times greater than 10 minutes simply add together the figures in the appropriate columns) | | | | | | | | | |
| | 1 keep warm low     2 | 25% | 150W | 4 | 8 | 12 | 16 | 20 | 24 | 28 | 32 | 36 | 40 |
| Low | 2 simmer     3 | 30% | 200W | 3¼ | 6¾ | 10 | 13¼ | 16¾ | 20 | 23¼ | 26¼ | 30 | 33¼ |
| Defrost | 3 stew    medium/low 4 | 40% | 250W | 2½ | 5 | 7½ | 10 | 12½ | 15 | 17½ | 20 | 22½ | 25 |
| | 4 defrost    medium    5 | 50% | 300W | 2 | 4 | 6 | 8 | 10 | 12 | 14 | 16 | 18 | 20 |
| Medium | 5 bake    medium    6 | 60% | 400W | 1¾ | 3¾ | 5 | 6¾ | 8¼ | 10 | 12 | 13¼ | 15 | 16½ |
| | 6 roast    high    7-8 | 75% | 500-500W | 1¼ | 2¾ | 4 | 5¼ | 6¾ | 8 | 9¼ | 10¾ | 12 | 13¼ |
| High | 7 full/high normal    10 | 100% | 700W | 1 | 2 | 3 | 4 | 5 | 6 | 7 | 8 | 9 | 10 |

# Vegetarian Menu Planning

If you are a long-standing vegetarian then you will have already discovered the best ways to serve a multitude of fresh and cooked foods for a nutritionally well-balanced diet. However, if you are a new convert to vegetarianism, or simply an infrequent meat-eater and want to serve more meat-free meals then you may welcome a little advice. It is often a frequent criticism of vegetarian food that it is difficult to know what to serve with what. Not so difficult with meat and two vegetables but when it is meat-free more puzzling.

It certainly is a question of familiarity and in time it seems simple to plan an exotic dinner for two, simple carefree lunch or nutritious mid-week supper the vegetarian way.

Practicalities to consider include texture, flavour, colour and

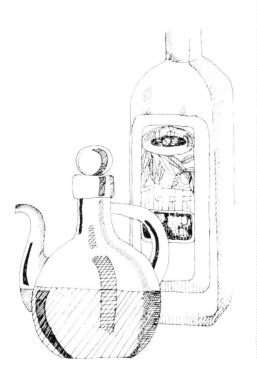

convenience but it is also important to consider dietary or nutritional requirements especially for the young and pregnant. In general terms, balance light starters and main courses with heartier puddings; or satisfying nibbles and a main course feast with a light dessert offering. Weigh main course 'anchors' like rice, pasta, potatoes and other grains or cereals with lighter vegetables, fruits, nuts, seeds and dairy produce - remembering at all times that variety is all-important.

A crisp seasonal salad is always welcome to add interest, texture and essential vitamins and minerals. However, don't make your menu planning a chore - use your refrigerator, freezer and chill cabinet to full effect alongside your microwave to produce meals in minutes that are full of goodness. Use the odd one or two convenience foods to supplement your diet but check labels carefully for ingredients. Use your supermarket fruit and salad counters to produce a variety of salads, fruit desserts and soup or casserole ingredients with no waste.

The following menus have been planned with the above considerations in mind and should provide a springboard or starting point for your own ideas:

## Late Breakfast or Lazy Sunday Brunch

## Curry Supper

## A Thai-Style Meal

## Eat in Chinese-Style

## Winter Soup and Salad Lunch

## Storecupboard Supper

## An Italian Experience

## Pauper's Feast

## Summer Lunch on the Terrace

## An Autumnal Dinner

## Middle Eastern Treat

## Cook or Make Ahead Menu

## Packed Lunch or Simple Picnic

## An Impressive Candlelit Meal for Two

## Sunday Lunch

*Mushrooms on Pesto Brioche Toast (page 25)*

# BRUNCHES, LUNCHES, STARTERS AND SNACKS

## *Piperade*

The microwave makes light work of this classic French dish of eggs with onion, pepper and tomato. Serve with toast fingers or wedges of crusty French or Farmhouse bread.

| One | | Two |
|---|---|---|
| 15 g/½ oz | butter | 25 g/1 oz |
| ½ small | green pepper, cored, seeded and chopped | 1 small |
| ½ small | onion, peeled and finely chopped | 1 small |
| ½ | clove of garlic, crushed | 1 |
| 2 | ripe tomatoes, skinned and coarsely chopped | 4 |
| 2 | eggs | 4 |
| | salt and pepper | |
| | parsley sprigs, to garnish | |

## One

1. Place the butter in a medium bowl and microwave on HIGH for 30 seconds, or until melted.

*Chilli Split Pea Dip with Warmed Pitta Wedges (page 40) and Falafels (page 48)*

2. Add the pepper, onion and garlic, mixing well. Cover and microwave on HIGH for 2½ - 3 minutes, stirring once halfway through the cooking time.

3. Stir in the tomatoes, mixing well. Cover and microwave on HIGH for 1 minute.

4. Meanwhile, beat the eggs with salt and pepper to taste then stir into the vegetable mixture. Microwave on HIGH for 1-2 minutes until the eggs are lightly scrambled, stirring every 30 seconds. Garnish with parsley and serve at once with toast fingers or wedges of crusty bread.

## Two

1. Place the butter in a medium bowl and microwave on HIGH for 45 seconds, or until melted.

2. Add the pepper, onion and garlic, mixing well. Cover and microwave on HIGH for 3 - 4 minutes, stirring once halfway through the cooking time.

3. Stir in the tomatoes, mixing well. Cover and microwave on HIGH for 1 minute.

4. Meanwhile, beat the eggs with salt and pepper to taste, then stir into the vegetable mixture. Microwave on HIGH for 2-3 minutes until the eggs are lightly scrambled, stirring every 30 seconds. Garnish with parsley and serve at once with toast fingers or wedges of crusty bread.

# *Bagels with Mushroom Scramble*

Soft, creamy scrambled eggs with the flavour of exotic mushrooms served on toasted bagels makes a wonderful Sunday brunch or light lunch dish.

| One | | Two |
|---|---|---|
| 15 g/½ oz | butter | 25 g/1 oz |
| 75 g/3 oz | assorted mushrooms | 175 g/6 oz |
| | (oyster, brown cap, shiitake and chanterelle, for example), wiped and sliced | |
| 2 | eggs | 4 |
| | salt and pepper | |
| 15 ml/1 tbsp | double cream | 30 ml/2 tbsp |
| 1 | bagels, halved and toasted | 2 |

## One

1. Place the butter in a medium bowl and microwave on HIGH for 15 seconds to melt. Add the mushrooms, mixing well. Cover and microwave on HIGH for 1-1½ minutes, stirring once until cooked and tender.

2. Meanwhile, beat the eggs with salt and pepper to taste. Stir into the mushroom mixture with the cream, mixing well.

3. Microwave on HIGH for 1 minute. Stir the set pieces of egg from the outside of the dish to the centre, then microwave on HIGH for a further 1-1½ minutes, stirring twice. Leave to stand for 1-2 minutes.

4. Place the bagel slices on a heated individual serving plate and spoon over the creamy mushroom scramble. Serve at once.

## Two

1. Place the butter in a medium bowl and microwave on HIGH for 30 seconds to melt. Add the mushrooms, mixing well. Cover and microwave on HIGH for 2-2½ minutes, stirring once until cooked and tender.

2. Meanwhile, beat the eggs with the salt and pepper to taste. Stir into the mushroom mixture with the cream, mixing well.

3. Microwave on HIGH for 1½ minutes. Stir the set pieces of egg from the outside of the dish to the centre, then microwave on HIGH for a further 1¼ - 2¼ minutes, stirring twice. Leave to stand for 1-2 minutes.

4. Divide the bagel slices between two heated individual serving plates and spoon the creamy mushroom scramble evenly over each. Serve at once.

# Raisin and Orange Muffins

My daughter Lucinda and son Charles love to have muffins for breakfast and brunch. This is a favourite recipe of theirs and makes 6. This is more than enough for one and ample for 2 but it really isn't worth making less. Anyway once sampled at breakfast you will probably want the rest for tea, failing that store in an airtight tin for the following day.

## To make six

| | |
|---|---|
| 37.5 ml/2½ tbsp | porridge oats |
| 50 g/2 oz | wholemeal flour |
| 15 ml/1 tbsp | oil |
| 30 ml/2 tbsp | caster sugar |
| | small pinch of salt |
| 25 g/1 oz | raisins |
| | 1 egg, beaten very lightly |
| | grated zest of ¼ orange |
| 5 ml/1 tsp | baking powder |
| 45 ml/3 tbsp | milk |

1. Mix the porridge oats with the flour. Add the oil, sugar, salt, raisins, egg and orange zest, mixing well.

2. Mix the baking powder with the milk, add to the raisin mixture and stir together quickly but do not beat.

3. Use the mixture to half-fill 6 double-thickness bun cases set in a microwave muffin tray or 6 ramekin dishes. Place the tray in the microwave or arrange the ramekins in a ring pattern on the microwave base and microwave on HIGH for 2½-3 minutes, rearranging once during the cooking time.

4. Place on a wire rack in their tray or ramekin dishes and leave to stand for 3 minutes. Remove from their paper cases when cool enough to handle. Serve warm or cold.

# Potato and Leek Pancakes

You'll need a browning dish to make this tasty potato pancake studded with green chopped leeks and chives. It makes a good light lunch dish or vegetable accompaniment.

| One | | Two |
|---|---|---|
| 1 | large baking potatoes, weighing about 225 g/8 oz | 2 |
| ½ | leek, cleaned and finely chopped | 1 |
| 10 ml/2 tsp | water | 20 ml/4 tsp |
| 10 ml/2 tsp | snipped chives | 20 ml/4 tsp |
| ½ | egg, beaten | 1 |
| 7.5 ml/1½ tsp | plain flour | 15 ml/1 tbsp |
| | salt and pepper | |
| 50 ml/2 fl oz | milk | 125 ml/4 fl oz |
| 15 ml/1 tbsp | vegetable oil | 15 ml/1 tbsp |

## One

1. Scrub the potato and prick well with a fork. Place in the microwave on a double thickness piece of absorbent kitchen paper and microwave on HIGH for 7-8 minutes or until soft, turning over once halfway through the cooking time. Leave to stand while cooking the leek.

2. Place the leek in a small bowl with the water. Cover tightly and microwave on HIGH for 1½-2 minutes until tender. Drain thoroughly.

3. Preheat a browning dish in the microwave on HIGH for 8-10 minutes (or according to the manufacturer's instructions).

4. Meanwhile, halve the potato and scoop the cooked flesh into a bowl. Add the chives, egg, flour and salt and pepper to taste. Mash well until smooth, then stir in the leek and milk, mixing well.

5. Add the oil to the browning dish and swirl to coat the bottom then quickly add the potato and leek mixture in a flat even layer to form a pancake. Microwave on HIGH for about 4-5 minutes or until firm.

6. Cut into wedges and remove from the dish with a spatula. Serve browned side uppermost.

## Two

1. Scrub the potatoes and prick well with a fork. Place in the microwave on a double thickness piece of absorbent kitchen paper and microwave on HIGH for 12 minutes or until soft, turning over once halfway through the cooking time. Leave to stand while cooking the leek.

2. Place the leek in a small bowl with the water. Cover tightly and microwave on HIGH for 2-3 minutes until tender. Drain thoroughly.

3. Preheat a browning dish in the microwave on HIGH for 8-10 minutes (or according to the manufacturer's instructions).

4. Meanwhile, halve the potato and scoop the cooked flesh into a bowl. Add the chives, egg, flour and salt and pepper to taste. Mash well until smooth, then stir in the leek and milk, mixing well.

5. Add the oil to the browning dish and swirl to coat the bottom then quickly add the potato and leek mixture in a flat even layer to form a pancake. Microwave on HIGH for about 7 minutes or until firm.

6. Cut into wedges and remove from the dish with a spatula. Divide evenly between two warmed serving plates and serve browned side uppermost.

# Spinach, Mushrooms and Eggs en Cocotte

It makes perfect sense to me to use a few cook's handy convenience foods alongside the microwave - especially when speed is of the essence. Canned creamed mushrooms when mixed with a dash of sherry can taste sublime when mixed and matched with spinach and eggs in this lunch, supper or snack dish.

| One | | Two |
|---|---|---|
| 30 ml/2 tbsp | chopped frozen spinach, thawed | 60 ml/4 tbsp |
| 30 ml/2 tbsp | canned creamed mushrooms | 60 ml/4 tbsp |
| 2.5-5 ml/½ - 1 tsp | dry sherry | 5-10 ml/1-2 tsp |
| | salt and pepper | |
| 1 | eggs | 2 |
| 15 ml/1 tbsp | double cream | 30 ml/2 tbsp |
| | parsley sprigs, to garnish | |
| | buttered toast, to serve | |

## One

1. Place the spinach in a bowl, cover tightly and microwave on HIGH for 1 minute or until hot.

2. Place the mushrooms in a small bowl with the sherry and salt and pepper to taste and microwave on HIGH for about 1 minute until hot, stirring once halfway through the cooking time.

3. Spoon the spinach mixture into a small (150 ml/¼ pt) ramekin dish and top with the creamed mushrooms. Make a small indentation in the centre of the mixture then crack in the egg. Gently prick the yolk in two places with a cocktail stick or the tip of a knife and microwave on MEDIUM for 1-1½ minutes or until the white is just set.

4. Spoon the cream over the egg and microwave on MEDIUM for 30 seconds. Leave to stand for 2 minutes before serving garnished with parsley sprigs. Serve while still hot with the buttered toast.

## Two

1. Place the spinach in a bowl, cover tightly and microwave on HIGH for 1-1½ minutes or until hot.

2. Place the mushrooms in a small bowl with the sherry and salt and pepper to taste and microwave on HIGH for about 1-1½ minutes until hot, stirring halfway through the cooking time.

3. Spoon the spinach mixture into two small (150 ml/¼ pt) ramekin dishes and top with the creamed mushrooms. Make a small indentation in the centre of the mixtures then crack in the eggs. Gently prick the yolks in two places with a cocktail stick or the tip of a knife and microwave on MEDIUM for 1½-2 minutes or until the whites are just set.

4. Spoon the cream over the eggs and microwave on MEDIUM for 45 seconds. Leave to stand for 2 minutes before serving garnished with parsley sprigs. Serve while still hot with the buttered toast.

# Mushrooms on Pesto Brioche Toast

This is a dish that I first sampled at the Malmaison Hotel et Brasserie in Edinburgh. I've adjusted it for microwave cooking and it's just as delicious.

| One | | Two |
|---|---|---|
| 30 ml/2 tbsp | olive oil | 60 ml/4 tbsp |
| 15 g/½ oz | butter | 25 g/1 oz |
| ¼ | clove of garlic, crushed | ½ |
| 100 g/4 oz | flat mushrooms, wiped | 225 g/8 oz |
| | salt and pepper | |
| 1 | large slices brioche | 2 |
| | pesto, for spreading | |
| | grated vegetarian Parmesan, for sprinkling | |
| ½ | sun-dried tomato, finely chopped | 1 |

## One

1. Place half of the oil and the butter in a medium bowl with the garlic, mushrooms and salt and pepper to taste. Cover tightly and microwave on HIGH for 2-3 minutes, stirring once until tender.

2. Meanwhile, toast the brioche and spread on one side with the pesto. Arrange the mushrooms over the top and sprinkle with the Parmesan cheese.

3. Mix the remaining oil with the tomato, drizzle over the top of the mushroom toast and serve at once.

## Two

1. Place half of the oil and the butter in a medium bowl with the garlic, mushrooms and salt and pepper to taste. Cover tightly and microwave on HIGH for 3-4 minutes, stirring once until tender.

2. Meanwhile, toast the brioche and spread on one side with the pesto. Divide between two individual warmed serving plates. Arrange the mushrooms on top of the toasted brioche and sprinkle with the Parmesan cheese.

3. Mix the remaining oil with the tomato, drizzle over the top of the mushroom toasts and serve at once.

# Vegetable-Plot Pasta Salad

Whether you have a vegetable plot or not, this is the recipe to turn the finest garden produce into a simple but sumptuous light summer pasta dish. Serve as part of a vegetarian buffet-style meal or as a light lunch dish.

| One | | Two |
|---|---|---|
| 50 g/2 oz | small dried pasta shells | 100 g/4 oz |
| 450 ml/¾ pt | boiling water | 600 ml/1 pt |
| 1 small | carrot, grated | 1 large |
| 2 | radishes, thinly sliced | 4 |
| 1 | baby courgettes, thinly sliced | 2 |
| 15 ml/1 tbsp | snipped chives | 30 ml/2 tbsp |
| 1.25 ml/¼ tsp | grated lemon zest | 2.5 ml/½ tsp |
| 10 ml/2 tsp | lemon juice | 22.5 ml/1½ tbsp |
| 15 ml/1 tbsp | olive oil | 30 ml/2 tbsp |
| | salt and pepper | |

## One and Two

1. Place the pasta in a large bowl with the boiling water and microwave on HIGH for 10-12 minutes, stirring once, until tender but still with some bite. Drain, rinse under cold running water, then drain again.

2. Meanwhile, mix the carrot with the radishes, courgette and chives.

3. Place the lemon zest and juice in a bowl then beat in the oil and salt and pepper to taste. Add to the pasta with the vegetable mixture and toss gently to mix. Allow to stand for 5-10 minutes to allow the flavours to develop before serving.

# Spring Vegetable Vinaigrette

Here is a colourful warm salad perfect for lunch or supper eating. Mix and match the vegetables according to what is available, remembering to give a good contrast of flavour, colour and texture for best results.

| One | | Two |
|---|---|---|
| 75 g/3 oz | baby new potatoes | 175 g/6 oz |
| 50 g/2 oz | baby carrots | 100 g/4 oz |
| 3 | dwarf corn | 6 |
| 45 ml/3 tbsp | water | 75 ml/5 tbsp |
| 50 g/2 oz | broccoli florets | 100 g/4 oz |
| 50 g/2 oz | mangetout | 100 g/4 oz |
| 1 | baby leeks | 2 |
| 40 g/1½ oz | cherry tomatoes | 75 g/3 oz |
| | Dressing: | |
| 30 ml/2 tbsp | olive oil | 60 ml/4 tbsp |
| ½ | clove of garlic, crushed | 1 |
| 2.5 ml/½ tsp | wholegrain mustard | 5 ml/1 tsp |
| 7.5 ml/1½ tsp | white wine vinegar | 15 ml/1 tbsp |
| 15 ml/1 tbsp | chopped fresh mixed herbs | 30 ml/2 tbsp |
| | salt and pepper | |

## One

1. Scrub the potatoes and carrots and place in a bowl with the corn and water. Cover and microwave on HIGH for 4 minutes.

2. Add the broccoli, mangetout and leeks, mixing well. Cover and microwave on HIGH for a further 2½ - 3 minutes until the vegetables are just tender crisp, stirring halfway through the cooking time. Drain well.

3. Meanwhile, to make the dressing, beat the oil with the garlic, mustard, vinegar and herbs. Season to taste with salt and pepper.

4. Add the cherry tomatoes and prepared dressing to the cooked vegetable mixture and toss gently to mix. Microwave on HIGH for 20 seconds. Leave to stand for 1 minute before serving.

## Two

1. Scrub the potatoes and carrots and place in a bowl with the corn and water. Cover and microwave on HIGH for 6 minutes.

2. Add the broccoli, mangetout and leeks, mixing well. Cover and microwave on HIGH for a further 4-5 minutes until the vegetables are just tender crisp, stirring halfway through the cooking time. Drain well.

3. Meanwhile, to make the dressing, beat the oil with the garlic, mustard, vinegar and herbs. Season to taste with salt and pepper.

4. Add the cherry tomatoes and prepared dressing to the cooked vegetable mixture and toss gently to mix. Microwave on HIGH for ½ minute. Leave to stand for 1 minute before serving.

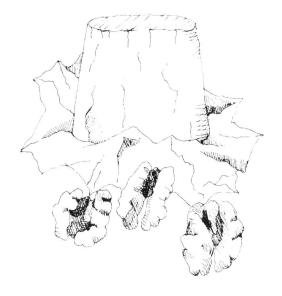

# *Warm Noodle Medley with Goat's Cheese*

I adore goat's cheese and find that its creamy texture and slightly sharp strong taste goes particularly well with bland Chinese egg noodles. When mixed with a sprinkling of herbs and scattering of nuts the dish is perfect for lunch, brunch or supper.

| One | | Two |
|---|---|---|
| 100 g/4 oz | Chinese dried egg noodles | 225 g/8 oz |
| 600 ml/1 pt | boiling water | 1.2 litres/2 pts |
| | salt and pepper | |
| 15 g/½ oz | butter or margarine | 25 g/1 oz |
| 30 ml/2 tbsp | double cream or crème fraîche | 60 ml/4 tbsp |
| 40 g/1½ oz | goat's cheese | 75 g/3 oz |
| 15 ml/1 tbsp | snipped chives | 30 ml/2 tbsp |
| 15-30 ml/ 1-2 tbsp | chopped toasted walnuts | 30-45 ml/ 2-3 tbsp |

## One

1. Place the noodles in a medium bowl with the boiling water and a pinch of salt. Stir well to soften the noodles and submerge them under the water. Cover loosely and microwave on HIGH for 3 minutes until almost tender. Remove from the microwave and leave to stand, covered, while preparing the sauce.

2. Place the butter and cream in a medium bowl and microwave on HIGH for 1-2 minutes, or until hot, stirring once halfway through the cooking time.

3. Crumble the goat's cheese and stir into the butter mixture until well blended. Add the chives and salt and pepper to taste, mixing well. Microwave on HIGH for 1 minute.

4. Drain the noodles thoroughly and add to the cheese mixture with the walnuts. Carefully toss the noodles to coat with the cheesy nut mixture. Microwave on HIGH for a further 1 minute until hot. Serve at once.

## Two

1. Place the noodles in a large bowl with the boiling water and a pinch of salt. Stir well to soften the noodles and submerge them under the water. Cover loosely and microwave on HIGH for 4 minutes until almost tender. Remove from the microwave and leave to stand, covered, while preparing the sauce.

2. Place the butter and cream in a large bowl and microwave on HIGH for 1½-2½ minutes, or until hot, stirring once halfway through the cooking time.

3. Crumble the goat's cheese and stir into the butter mixture until well blended. Add the chives and salt and pepper to taste, mixing well. Microwave on HIGH for 1½ minutes.

4. Drain the noodles thoroughly and add to the cheese mixture with the walnuts. Carefully toss the noodles to coat with the cheesy nut mixture. Microwave on HIGH for a further 1-1½ minutes until hot. Serve at once.

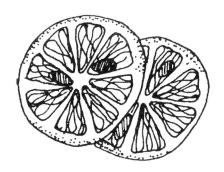

# Vegetarian Gado Gado

In this recipe peppers, broccoli and mangetout are tossed with rice in a flavoursome sauce made with peanut butter, ginger, garlic, onion and soy sauce. It makes a splendid light lunch dish or can be used as part of a cold buffet selection of salads.

| One | | Two |
|---|---|---|
| ¼ | onion, peeled and finely sliced | ½ |
| ½ | clove of garlic, crushed | 1 |
| 5 ml/1 tsp | vegetable oil | 10 ml/2 tsp |
| 5 ml/1 tsp | soy sauce | 10 ml/2 tsp |
| | pinch of dried red pepper flakes | |
| | dash of lemon juice | |
| 2.5 ml/½ tsp | ground ginger | 5 ml/1 tsp |
| 45 ml/3 tbsp | vegetable stock | 90 ml/6 tbsp |
| 15 ml/1 tbsp | creamy peanut butter | 30 ml/2 tbsp |
| 50 g/2 oz | mangetout, trimmed | 100 g/4 oz |
| 50 g/2 oz | small broccoli florets | 100 g/4 oz |
| 15 ml/1 tbsp | water | 30 ml/2 tbsp |
| 75 g/3 oz | cooked long grain rice | 175 g/6 oz |
| ¼ | red pepper, cored, seeded and finely sliced | ½ |
| | salt and pepper | |

## One

1. Place the onion, garlic and oil in a small bowl and microwave on HIGH for 45 seconds. Add the soy sauce, red pepper flakes, lemon juice, ginger and stock, mixing well. Microwave on HIGH for a

further 30 seconds. Whisk in the peanut butter and leave to stand while preparing the vegetables.

2. Place the mangetout and broccoli in a bowl with the water. Cover tightly and microwave on HIGH for 2 minutes until almost tender and still crisp. Leave to stand for 2 minutes, then drain thoroughly.

3. Meanwhile, microwave the peanut butter mixture on HIGH for 1-2 minutes, stirring twice until the mixture is hot, bubbly and slightly thickened.

4. Mix the rice with the cooked broccoli and mangetout. Add the red pepper, cooked sauce and salt and pepper to taste. Toss well to mix. Serve warm or cold.

## Two

1. Place the onion, garlic and oil in a medium bowl and microwave on HIGH for 1 minute. Add the soy sauce, red pepper flakes, lemon juice, ginger and stock, mixing well. Microwave on HIGH for a further 45 seconds. Whisk in the peanut butter and leave to stand while preparing the vegetables.

2. Place the mangetout and broccoli in a bowl with the water. Cover tightly and microwave on HIGH for 3 minutes until almost tender and still crisp. Leave to stand for 2 minutes, then drain thoroughly.

3. Meanwhile, microwave the peanut butter mixture on HIGH for 1½-2¼ minutes, stirring twice until the mixture is hot and bubbly and slightly thickened.

4. Mix the rice with the cooked broccoli and mangetout. Add the red pepper, cooked sauce and salt and pepper to taste. Toss well to mix. Serve warm or cold.

# Warm Red Salad

I love to make this salad in the winter months for a lunchtime treat or lazy supper dish - with red onions, red potatoes, cheese and a tangy dressing it has all the makings of a feast.

| One | | Two |
|---|---|---|
| 175 g/6 oz | small red potatoes, scrubbed and halved if more than bite-sized | 350 g/12 oz |
| 30 ml/2 tbsp | water | 60 ml/4 tbsp |
| 22.5 ml/1½ tbsp | olive oil | 45 ml/3 tbsp |
| ½ | red onion, peeled and thinly sliced | 1 |
| 10 ml/2 tsp | chopped fresh thyme | 20 ml/4 tsp |
| 7.5 ml/1½ tsp | balsamic vinegar | 15 ml/1 tbsp |
| 2.5 ml/½ tsp | dark soy sauce | 5 ml/1 tsp |
| | salt and pepper | |
| 25 g/1 oz | assorted salad leaves | 50 g/2 oz |
| 50 g/2 oz | vegetarian semi-hard cheese, shaved into curly pieces | 100 g/4 oz |

## One

1. Place the potatoes in a bowl with the water. Cover and microwave on HIGH for 3-4 minutes, stirring once, until just tender. Leave to stand, covered, for 5 minutes before draining thoroughly.

2. Meanwhile, place the oil, onion and thyme in a bowl, cover and microwave on HIGH for 2 minutes, stirring once.

3. Add the vinegar, soy sauce and salt and pepper to taste, mixing well. Add the drained potatoes and toss gently to mix.

4. Place the salad leaves in a shallow serving bowl and spoon over the hot potato and onion mixture (the leaves will wilt slightly during this stage). Sprinkle with the shaved cheese and serve at once.

## Two

1. Place the potatoes in a bowl with the water. Cover and microwave on HIGH for 5-7 minutes, stirring once, until just tender. Leave to stand, covered, for 5 minutes before draining thoroughly.

2. Meanwhile, place the oil, onion and thyme in a bowl, cover and microwave on HIGH for 3 minutes, stirring once.

3. Add the vinegar, soy sauce and salt and pepper to taste, mixing well. Add the drained potatoes and toss gently to mix.

4. Place the salad leaves in two shallow serving bowls and spoon over the potato and onion mixture equally (the leaves will wilt slightly at this stage). Sprinkle with the shaved cheese and serve at once.

# Warm Mushroom and Rocket Salad

This warm salad medley of mixed mushrooms and crisp rocket leaves makes a wonderful light lunch dish or quick and easy starter to a special dinner party meal. Serve with an interesting bread to mop up the juices if you like.

| One | | Two |
|---|---|---|
| 25 g/1 oz | rocket leaves | 50 g/2 oz |
| 15 g/ ½ oz | butter or margarine | 25 g/1 oz |
| ½ | small shallot, finely chopped | 1 |
| ½ | clove of garlic, crushed | 1 |
| 50 g/2 oz | mixed mushrooms (shiitake, chanterelle and oyster, for example), wiped | 100 g/4 oz |
| 7.5 ml/1 ½ tsp | balsamic vinegar | 15 ml/1 tbsp |
| 15 g/ ½ oz | toasted pinenuts | 25 g/1 oz |
| | salt and pepper | |
| | chopped fresh parsley, to garnish | |

## One

1. Arrange the rocket leaves on an individual serving plate and chill well.

2. Place the butter or margarine, shallot and garlic in a medium-sized bowl and microwave on HIGH for 45-60 seconds, stirring once.

3. Add the mushrooms (cutting any that are large into bite-sized pieces) and toss in the buttery mixture to coat. Cover and microwave on HIGH for 1-1½ minutes, stirring once, until the mushrooms are just cooked.

4. Add the balsamic vinegar, pinenuts and salt and pepper to taste, mixing well. Spoon over the rocket leaves, sprinkle with chopped parsley and serve at once.

## Two

1. Arrange the rocket leaves on two individual serving plates and chill well.

2. Place the butter or margarine, shallot and garlic in a medium-sized bowl and microwave on HIGH for 1-1¼ minutes, stirring once.

3. Add the mushrooms (cutting any that are large into bite-sized pieces) and toss in the buttery mixture to coat. Cover and microwave on HIGH for 2-2½ minutes, stirring once, until the mushrooms are just cooked.

4. Add the balsamic vinegar, pinenuts and salt and pepper to taste, mixing well. Spoon equally over the rocket leaves, sprinkle with chopped parsley and serve at once.

## *Vegetarian Caesar Salad*

For best results this salad should be made with roasted yellow peppers. The best way to do this is under the grill. Halve and core the peppers and grill, skin side up, for 10-15 minutes until the skin is blistered and blackened. Cover with a tea-towel and leave to cool slightly, then peel away the skin - it will come away very easily. Cut into long strips for use.

| One | | Two |
|---|---|---|
| 15 g/½ oz | butter | 25 g/1 oz |
| 5 ml/1 tsp | olive oil | 10 ml/2 tsp |
| 1 | large slices bread, crusts removed and cut into cubes | 2 |
| 15 ml/1 tbsp | mayonnaise | 30 ml/2 tbsp |
| ½ | clove of garlic, crushed | 1 |
| 10 ml/2 tsp | grated vegetarian Parmesan cheese | 20 ml/4 tsp |
| 10-15 ml/2-3 tsp | water | 20-30 ml/4-6 tsp |
| | salt and pepper | |
| 25 g/1 oz | assorted salad leaves | 50 g/2 oz |
| 1 | medium yellow peppers, grilled as above and cut into thin strips | 2 |
| 10 ml/2 tsp | shaved fresh vegetarian Parmesan cheese | 20 ml/4 tsp |

## One

1. Place the butter and oil in a large shallow dish and microwave on HIGH for 30 seconds. Add the bread cubes and toss to coat. Microwave on HIGH for 1-2 minutes, stirring every 30 seconds until the croûtons are crisp and brown. Drain on absorbent kitchen paper. Keep warm.

2. To make the dressing, place the mayonnaise, garlic, grated Parmesan, water and salt and pepper to taste in a blender or food processor and blend until smooth. Alternatively whisk together in a small bowl until smooth.

3. Line an individual serving plate with the salad leaves and scatter over the pepper slices.

4. Add the hot crispy croûtons, drizzle over the dressing and sprinkle with the shaved Parmesan. Serve at once.

## Two

1. Place the butter and oil in a large shallow dish and microwave on HIGH for 30 seconds. Add the bread cubes and toss to coat. Microwave on HIGH for 1½ - 2½ minutes, stirring every 30 seconds until the croûtons are crisp and brown. Drain on absorbent kitchen paper. Keep warm.

2. To make the dressing, place the mayonnaise, garlic, grated Parmesan, water and salt and pepper to taste in a blender or food processor and blend until smooth.

3. Line two individual serving plates with an equal quantity of the salad leaves and scatter the pepper slices equally over each.

4. Add the hot crispy croûtons, drizzle over the dressing and sprinkle with the shaved Parmesan. Serve at once.

# Mushroom, Thyme and Sherry Soup

Here is a soup that is special enough to serve to guests for dinner or to eat alone when one needs a little pampering!

| One | | Two |
| --- | --- | --- |
| 7 g/¼ oz | butter | 15 g/½ oz |
| ¼ | onion, chopped | ½ |
| 7 g/¼ oz | plain flour | 15 g/½ oz |
| 175 g/6 oz | mixed mushrooms, wiped and sliced | 350 g/12 oz |
| 1 | sprigs of thyme | 2 |
| 150 ml/¼ pt | hot vegetable stock | 300 ml/½ pt |
| 10 ml/2 tsp | dry sherry | 20 ml/4 tsp |
| 45 ml/3 tbsp | single cream | 90 ml/6 tbsp |
| | salt and pepper | |

## One

1. Place the butter and onion in a large bowl. Cover and microwave on HIGH for 1 minute. Stir in the flour and microwave on HIGH for a further 30 seconds.

2. Add the mushrooms with the thyme sprig, then gradually stir in the hot stock, mixing well. Cover and microwave on HIGH for 3 minutes, stirring once.

3. Remove and discard the thyme sprig and stir in the sherry. Transfer to a blender or food processor and purée until smooth.

4. Return to the bowl, add the cream and season with salt and pepper to taste. Microwave on HIGH for 30 seconds to reheat. Serve hot.

## Two

1. Place the butter and onion in a large bowl. Cover and microwave on HIGH for 1½ minutes. Stir in the flour and microwave on HIGH for a further 30 seconds.

2. Add the mushrooms with the thyme sprigs, then gradually stir in the hot stock, mixing well. Cover and microwave on HIGH for 5-6 minutes, stirring once.

3. Remove and discard the thyme sprigs and stir in the sherry. Transfer to a blender or food processor and purée until smooth.

4. Return to the bowl, add the cream and season with salt and pepper to taste. Microwave on HIGH for 45 seconds to reheat. Serve hot.

# Pumpkin and Carrot Soup with Croûtons

This warming, autumnal soup is just the thing to make around Hallow'een when the scooped out flesh of pumpkin lanterns begs to be used.

| One | | Two |
|---|---|---|
| 75 g/3 oz | carrots, peeled and thinly sliced | 175 g/6 oz |
| 100 g/4 oz | pumpkin flesh, finely chopped | 225 g/8 oz |
| 125 ml/4 fl oz | hot vegetable stock | 50 ml/8 fl oz |
| 15 g/½ oz | butter or margarine | 25 g/1 oz |
| 1.25 ml/¼ tsp | paprika | 2.5 ml/½ tsp |
| | salt and grated nutmeg | |
| 30 ml/2 tbsp | double cream or crème fraîche | 60 ml/4 tbsp |
| | croûtons, to serve | |

## One

1. Place the carrots and the pumpkin in a small dish. Cover tightly and microwave on HIGH for 4-4½ minutes until tender.

2. Place in a blender or food processor with the stock, butter, paprika and salt and nutmeg to taste. Process until smooth.

3. Return to a serving dish or jug and stir in the cream or crème fraîche. Cover and microwave on HIGH for 2 minutes, stirring once.

4. Serve hot sprinkled with croûtons.

## Two

1. Place the carrots and pumpkin in a medium dish. Cover tightly and microwave on HIGH for 6-7 minutes until tender.

2. Place in a blender or food processor with the stock, butter, paprika and salt and nutmeg to taste. Process until smooth.

3. Return to a jug and stir in the cream or crème fraîche. Cover and microwave on HIGH for 3 minutes, stirring once.

4. Pour into two individual serving bowls and serve hot, sprinkled with croûtons.

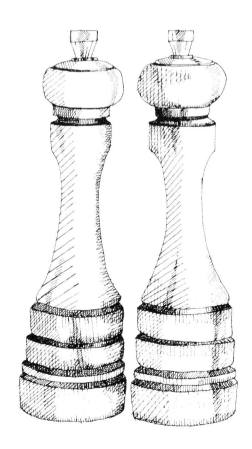

# West Country Soup

This is a rich, creamy soup made with cheese and cider reminiscent of mellow Somerset, yet spiked with a little horseradish for an added kick. Serve with warm crusty bread for lunch, supper or a hearty snack.

| One | | Two |
|---|---|---|
| ¼ | onion, finely chopped | ½ |
| 7 g/¼ oz | butter or margarine | 15 g/½ oz |
| 75 ml/5 tbsp | dry cider | 150 ml/¼ pt |
| 10 ml/2 tsp | creamed horseradish | 20 ml/4 tsp |
| 50 g/2 oz | vegetarian Cheddar cheese, grated | 100 g/4 oz |
| 11.25 ml/2¼ tsp | plain flour | 22.5 ml/1½ tbsp |
| 75 ml/5 tbsp | hot vegetable stock | 150 ml/¼ pt |
| | salt and pepper | |
| 37.5 ml/2½ tbsp | single cream | 75 ml/5 tbsp |
| 15 ml/1 tbsp | chopped parsley | 30 ml/2 tbsp |

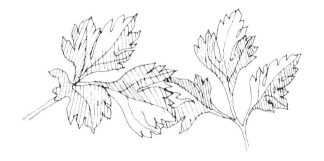

## One

1. Place the onion and butter or margarine in a medium bowl and microwave on HIGH for 1 minute.

2. Add the cider and horseradish, mixing well. Microwave on HIGH for 1½ minutes.

3. Meanwhile, mix the cheese with the flour then gradually whisk into the cider mixture, a little at a time. Microwave on HIGH for 1½-2 minutes, whisking halfway through the cooking time.

4. Whisk in the vegetable stock with salt and pepper to taste and the cream. Microwave on HIGH for 45-60 seconds to reheat.

5. Pour into a warmed serving bowl and sprinkle with the parsley to serve. Serve with warm crusty bread.

## Two

1. Place the onion and butter or margarine in a medium bowl and microwave on HIGH for 2 minutes.

2. Add the cider and horseradish, mixing well. Microwave on HIGH for 2-3 minutes.

3. Meanwhile, mix the cheese with the flour then gradually whisk into the cider mixture, a little at a time. Microwave on HIGH for 3-3½ minutes, whisking halfway through the cooking time.

4. Whisk in the vegetable stock with salt and pepper to taste and the cream. Microwave on HIGH for 1-1½ minutes to reheat.

5. Pour into two warmed individual serving bowls and sprinkle with the parsley to serve. Serve with warm crusty bread.

# Wild Mushroom Platter with Melted Goat's Cheese

It isn't difficult any more to find the more unusual wild mushrooms that are used in this dish, most supermarkets flaunt a wide selection. You can, of course, use cultivated mushrooms too but be extravagant with your selection including oyster, ceps and shiitake to give a contrast of flavours and textures. Serve with herbed bread or New Wave Garlic Bread (see page 110) for a light meal.

| One | | Two |
|---|---|---|
| 5 ml/1 tsp | olive oil | 10 ml/2 tsp |
| 2 | spring onions, sliced | 4 |
| ½ | clove of garlic, crushed | 1 |
| 50 g/2 oz | mixed wild mushrooms, wiped and sliced or broken into bite-sized pieces | 100 g/4 oz |
| 20 g/¾ oz | toasted pine nuts | 40 g/1½ oz |
| 15 ml/1 tbsp | chopped fresh basil | 30 ml/2 tbsp |
| | salt and pepper | |
| 50 g/2 oz | cylinder-shaped piece of goat's cheese | 100 g/4 oz |
| | herbed French bread or New Wave Garlic Bread (see page 110) to serve | |

## One

1. Place the oil, spring onions, garlic and mushrooms in a medium bowl, cover tightly and microwave on HIGH for about 1 minute, stirring once halfway through the cooking time, until tender.

2. Add the pine nuts, basil and salt and pepper to taste, blending well. Spoon on to a warmed individual serving plate.

3. Slice the goat's cheese thickly into 2-3 pieces and overlap on top of the mushroom mixture. Microwave on HIGH for about 30-45 seconds or until the cheese just begins to melt.

4. Serve at once with herbed French bread or New Wave Garlic Bread.

## Two

1. Place the oil, spring onions, garlic and mushrooms in a medium bowl, cover tightly and microwave on HIGH for 1-1½ minutes, stirring once halfway through the cooking time, until tender.

2. Add the pine nuts, basil and salt and pepper to taste, blending well. Spoon on to two small individual serving plates.

3. Slice the goat's cheese thickly into 4-6 pieces and overlap on top of the mushroom mixture. Microwave both plates in the oven on HIGH for about 1 minute or until the cheese just begins to melt.

4. Serve at once with herbed French bread or New Wave Garlic Bread.

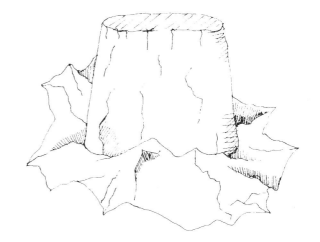

# Noodles with South Seas Salsa

A salsa takes just minutes to make and noodles take just minutes to cook. Mix them together and you have a wonderful light meal for 1 or 2.

## One | | Two

| One | | Two |
|---|---|---|
| 100 g/4 oz | dried egg noodles | 225 g/8 oz |
| | salt and pepper | |
| 600 ml/1 pt | boiling water | 1.2 litres/2 pts |
| 100 g/4 oz | ripe tomatoes | 225 g/8 oz |
| 2 | spring onions, chopped | 4 |
| 15 ml/1 tbsp | chopped fresh basil | 30 ml/2 tbsp |
| 15 ml/1 tbsp | chopped fresh mint | 30 ml/2 tbsp |
| 15 ml/1 tbsp | chopped fresh coriander | 30 ml/2 tbsp |
| ½ | clove of garlic, crushed | 1 |
| 10 ml/2 tsp | lime juice | 20 ml/4 tsp |
| 7.5 ml/1 ½ tsp | sunflower oil | 15 ml/1 tbsp |
| 7.5 ml/1 ½ tsp | soy sauce or Thai fish sauce | 15 ml/1 tbsp |
| 5 ml/1 tsp | light brown sugar | 10 ml/2 tsp |
| 1.25-2.5 ml/ ¼ -½ tsp | Chinese chilli sauce | 2.5-3.75 ml/ ½ -¾ tsp |

## One and Two

1. Place the noodles, salt to taste and the boiling water in a medium bowl and stir well. Cover and microwave on HIGH for 3-4 minutes, or until almost tender, stirring every 1 minute. Leave to stand, covered, while preparing the salsa.

2. To make the salsa, skin the tomatoes, if you like, then remove the seeds. Finely chop the tomatoes and mix with the spring onions. Add the herbs, garlic, lime juice, oil, soy or fish sauce, sugar, chilli sauce and salt and pepper to taste. Mix well to combine thoroughly.

3. Drain the noodles, add the prepared salsa and mix together with two forks. Serve at once. If the noodles need reheating then microwave on HIGH for 1-2 minutes until hot.

# Muffin Rarebit

Cheese on toast has to be one of the easiest and most substantial snacks around. Here the microwave makes light work of melting cheese with seasonings to top a toasted muffin.

| One | | Two |
|---|---|---|
| 50 ml/2 fl oz | beer | 125 ml/4 fl oz |
| 7 g/¼ oz | butter | 15 g/½ oz |
| 2.5 ml/½ tsp | Worcestershire sauce | 5 ml/1 tsp |
| pinch | mustard powder | 1.25 ml/¼ tsp |
| 100 g/4 oz | vegetarian Cheddar cheese, grated | 225 g/8 oz |
| 7.5 ml/1 ½ tsp | plain flour | 15 ml/1 tbsp |
| 1 | muffins, split | 2 |

## One

1. Mix the beer with the butter, Worcestershire sauce and mustard powder in a medium bowl. Microwave on HIGH for 2 minutes, or until the mixture boils and the butter has melted.

2. Meanwhile, mix the cheese with the flour then gradually stir into the beer mixture, mixing well.

*Warm Broad Bean, Lemon Olive and Mozzarella Salad
(page 66) and Microwave Roasted Garlic (page 85)*

3. Reduce the power setting to MEDIUM and cook for 1-2 minutes, or until the cheese melts and the mixture is smooth and creamy, whisking every 1 minute.

4. Meanwhile, toast the muffin and place on a warmed serving plate. Pour over the cheese mixture and serve at once.

## Two

1. Mix the beer with the butter, Worcestershire sauce and mustard powder in a large bowl. Microwave on HIGH for 2½-3 minutes, or until the mixture boils and the butter has melted.

2. Meanwhile, mix the cheese with the flour then gradually stir into the beer mixture, mixing well.

3. Reduce the power setting to MEDIUM and cook for 2-2½ minutes, or until the cheese melts and the mixture is smooth and creamy, whisking every 1 minute.

4. Meanwhile, toast the muffins and place on two warmed serving plates. Pour the cheese mixture evenly over the muffins and serve at once.

*Summer Vegetable Bonanza (page 45) with Vegetarian Caesar Salad (page 31)*

# Lentil and Sun-Soaked Dried Tomato Pâté

This creamy lentil pâté flavoured with very finely chopped sun-dried tomatoes must be served very well chilled for best results. Serve with crisp toast, crackers or, my favourite, pumpernickel bread.

| One | | Two |
|---|---|---|
| ¼ | onion, peeled and finely chopped | ½ |
| 7 g/¼ oz | butter or margarine | 15 g/½ oz |
| 50 g/2 oz | lentils | 100 g/4 oz |
| | salt and pepper | |
| 150 ml/¼ pt | water or vegetable stock | 300 ml/½ pt |
| ¼ | grated rind of lemon | ½ |
| 5 ml/1 tsp | snipped chives | 10 ml/2 tsp |
| 5 ml/1 tsp | finely chopped sun-dried tomatoes in oil | 10 ml/2 tsp |
| 25 g/1 oz | full-fat soft or cream cheese | 50 g/2 oz |

## One

1. Place the onion in a bowl with the butter or margarine and microwave on HIGH for 1 minute.

2. Add the lentils and salt and pepper to taste, mixing well, then stir in the water or stock. Cover and microwave on HIGH for 15 minutes, stirring once and adding a little more stock or water if the mixture becomes too dry.

3. Mash the cooked lentils with a fork until almost smooth then beat in the lemon rind. Cover and microwave on HIGH for a further 5 minutes.

4. Add the chives, tomatoes and cheese, beating well until well blended. Transfer to a small serving dish, cool then chill thoroughly before serving.

## Two

1. Place the onion in a bowl with the butter or margarine and microwave on HIGH for 1½-2 minutes until softened.

2. Add the lentils and salt and pepper to taste, mixing well, then stir in the water or stock. Cover and microwave on HIGH for 15 minutes, stirring once and adding a little more stock or water if the mixture becomes too dry.

3. Mash the cooked lentils with a fork until almost smooth then beat in the lemon rind. Cover and microwave on HIGH for a further 5 minutes.

4. Add the chives, tomatoes and cheese, beating well until well blended. Transfer to a small bowl or two individual serving dishes, cool then chill thoroughly before serving.

# Chestnut, Blue Cheese and Chive Pâté

This is a superb well-flavoured pâté all the better for serving with toasted crusty bread or crisp crackers. Chill well, for at least 4 hours before scooping to serve.

| One | | Two |
| --- | --- | --- |
| 1 | shallots, finely chopped | 2 |
| 5 ml/1 tsp | brandy | 10 ml/2 tsp |
| ½ | 220 g/7 oz can unsweetened chestnut purée | 1 |
| 50 g/2 oz | Gorgonzola or soft blue cheese | 100 g/4 oz |
| 15 ml/1 tbsp | snipped chives | 30 ml/2 tbsp |
| 15 g/½ oz | cooked, peeled chestnuts, coarsely chopped | 25 g/1 oz |
| | salt and pepper | |

## One

1. Place the shallot and brandy in a small bowl, cover and microwave on HIGH for 45 seconds or until the shallot is tender.

2. Place in a food processor or blender with the chestnut purée and soft blue cheese. Purée until soft and well combined.

3. Remove form the processor and blender and add the chives, chestnuts and salt and pepper to taste, mixing thoroughly before serving.

## Two

1. Place the shallots and brandy in a small bowl, cover and microwave on HIGH for 1 minute or until the shallots are tender.

2. Place in a food processor or blender with the chestnut purée and soft blue cheese. Purée until soft and well combined.

3. Remove from the processor and blender and add the chives, chestnuts and salt and pepper to taste, mixing thoroughly before serving.

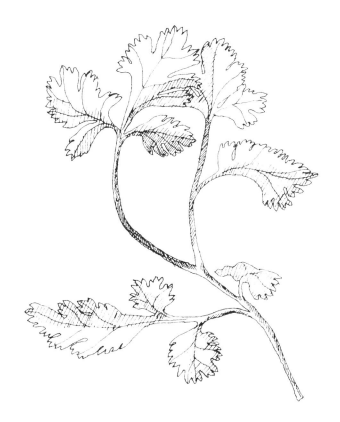

# *Middle Eastern Aubergine Dip with Veggie Sticks*

This is just the dip to make for serving with drinks or a light snack dish for mid-day or mid-way eating. The veggie sticks can be replaced with warm strips of pitta or flat bread for a more substantial dish if you prefer.

| One | | Two |
|---|---|---|
| ½ | small aubergine | 1 |
| 7.5 ml/1½ tsp | extra-virgin olive oil | 15 ml/1 tbsp |
| 1.25 ml/¼ tsp | ground cumin | 2.5 ml/½ tsp |
| 1.25 ml/¼ tsp | ground coriander | 2.5 ml/½ tsp |
| pinch | mild chilli powder | 1.25 ml/¼ tsp |
| ½ | clove of garlic, crushed | 1 |
| 5 ml/1 tsp | lime juice | 10 ml/2 tsp |
| 75 ml/5 tbsp | natural yogurt | 150 ml/¼ pt |
| 5 ml/1 tsp | chopped fresh parsley | 10 ml/2 tsp |
| 2.5 ml/½ tsp | chopped fresh coriander | 5 ml/1 tsp |
| | salt and pepper | |
| 175 g/6 oz | assorted prepared | 350 g/12 oz |
| | **vegetable sticks to serve (carrot julienne, baby mushrooms, cherry tomatoes, cucumber and celery batons and pepper strips for example)** | |

## One

1. Prick the aubergine several times with a fork and place in the microwave on a double thickness sheet of absorbent kitchen paper. Microwave on HIGH for 3–3½ minutes or until very soft. Leave to stand until cool enough to handle.

2. Meanwhile, place the oil in a medium bowl with the spices and garlic, mixing well. Microwave on HIGH for 1–1½ minutes, stirring twice, to cook the spices. Add the lime juice and mix well.

3. Halve the aubergine and carefully scoop out the cooked flesh into the spice mixture. Beat well with a fork to break down the flesh to make a fairly smooth purée.

4. Add the yogurt a spoonful at a time, then beat in the parsley, coriander and salt and pepper to taste.

5. To serve, spoon the aubergine dip into a small bowl, place on a serving plate and surround with the crisp vegetable stick selection.

## Two

1. Prick the aubergine several times with a fork and place in the microwave on a double thickness sheet of absorbent kitchen paper. Microwave on HIGH for 4–5 minutes or until very soft. Leave to stand until cool enough to handle.

2. Meanwhile, place the oil in a medium bowl with the spices and garlic, mixing well. Microwave on HIGH for 2 minutes, stirring twice, to cook the spices. Add the lime juice and mix well.

3. Halve the aubergine and carefully scoop out the cooked flesh into the spice mixture. Beat well with a fork to break down the flesh to make a fairly smooth purée.

4. Add the yogurt, a spoonful at a time, then beat in the parsley, coriander and salt and pepper to taste.

5. To serve, spoon the aubergine dip into a medium bowl, place on a serving plate and surround with the crisp vegetable stick selection. Alternatively, divide the mixture between two bowls and plates for individual presentation.

# Chilli Split Pea Dip with Warmed Pitta Wedges

I always make double the quantity of this dip for myself since it is so moreish. It's rather like a lemony hummus and is delicious when served with warmed pitta but also terrific with veggie sticks.

| One | | Two |
|---|---|---|
| 50 g/2 oz | yellow split peas, soaked overnight in cold water | 100 g/4 oz |
| | boiling water to cover | |
| 10 ml/2 tsp | extra-virgin olive oil | 20 ml/4 tsp |
| ¼ | grated zest and juice of lemon | ½ |
| ½ | small clove of garlic, crushed | 1 |
| ½ | small green chilli, seeded and very finely chopped | 1 |
| | salt and pepper | |
| 1-2 | pitta breads | 2-4 |

## One and Two

1. Rinse and drain the split peas and place in a medium dish then pour over sufficient boiling water to cover. Cover and microwave on HIGH for 10 minutes, stirring once, until soft. Drain thoroughly.

2. Place the drained split peas in a blender or food processor with the oil, lemon zest, lemon juice and garlic. Purée to a soft consistency. Add a little more lemon juice if the mixture is too stiff.

3. Add the chilli and salt and pepper to taste, mixing well. Spoon into a small bowl and chill until ready to serve.

4. Place the bread on a plate lined with a double thickness piece of absorbent kitchen paper and microwave on HIGH for 10-30 seconds, depending upon number or until warm. Slice into wedges or fingers and serve while still warm with the split pea dip.

# Jacket Potatoes with Pastures New Filling

These are jacket potatoes with a big difference - they have a tasty filling of herbed mushrooms instead of the usual soured cream, butter or grated cheese. Savour for lunch or a speedy supper dish.

| One | | Two |
|---|---|---|
| 1 | baking potatoes, weighing about 225 g/8 oz | 2 |
| 15 g/½ oz | butter or margarine | 25 g/1 oz |
| ½ | small clove of garlic, crushed | 1 |
| 5 ml/1 tsp | chopped fresh parsley | 10 ml/2 tsp |
| | pinch of dried thyme | |
| 3.75 ml/¾ tsp | wholegrain mustard | 7.5 ml/1½ tsp |
| 60 g/2½ oz | mushrooms, wiped and sliced | 150 g/5 oz |
| | salt and pepper | |

## One

1. Scrub the potato, prick the skin with a fork and place on a double thickness sheet of absorbent kitchen paper and microwave on HIGH for 6-7 minutes, turning over once, until tender and soft to the squeeze. Wrap in foil and leave to stand while preparing the filling.

2. Place the butter or margarine in a bowl and mix with the garlic, parsley, thyme and mustard. Add the mushrooms with salt and pepper to taste. Cover and microwave on HIGH for 1-1½ minutes, stirring once.

3. Remove the potato from the foil and make a crosswise cut on the top. Protecting your hand with an oven glove, squeeze the base of the potato so that the top opens out. Fill with the hot mushroom mixture and serve at once.

## Two

1. Scrub the potatoes, prick the skins with a fork and place on a double thickness piece of absorbent

kitchen paper and microwave on HIGH for 10-12 minutes, turning over once, until tender and soft to the squeeze. Wrap in foil and leave to stand while preparing the filling.

2. Place the butter or margarine in a bowl and mix with the garlic, parsley, thyme and mustard. Add the mushrooms with salt and pepper to taste. Cover and microwave on HIGH for 1½-2 minutes, stirring once.

3. Remove the potatoes from the foil and make a crosswise cut on the top of each. Protecting your hand with an oven glove, squeeze the base of each potato so that the top opens out. Fill with an equal quantity of the hot mushroom mixture and serve at once.

# *Blue Brie, Mushroom and Chive Jackets*

Any vegetarian soft blue cheese can be used to make the filling for this jacket-baked potato but blue brie works particularly well.

| One | | Two |
|---|---|---|
| 1 | baking potatoes, weighing about 225 g/8 oz | 2 |
| 25 g/1 oz | mushrooms, wiped and sliced | 50 g/2 oz |
| 15 g/½ oz | butter | 25 g/1 oz |
| 50 g/2 oz | vegetarian blue brie | 100 g/4 oz |
| 10 ml/2 tsp | snipped fresh chives | 20 ml/4 tsp |
| | salt and pepper | |

## One

1. Scrub the potato, prick the skin with a fork and place on a double thickness sheet of absorbent kitchen paper and microwave on HIGH for 6-7 minutes, turning over once, until tender and soft to the squeeze. Wrap in foil and leave to stand while preparing the filling.

2. Place the mushrooms in a bowl with the butter. Cover and microwave on HIGH for 30-60 seconds, stirring once.

3. Thinly pare the rind from the brie and discard. Cut the brie into bite-sized cubes.

4. Unwrap the potato and cut in half. Scoop out the cooked flesh into a bowl. Add the mushrooms and their juice, the brie, chives and salt and pepper to taste. Mix gently and return to the potato shells.

5. Place on a serving plate and microwave on HIGH for 15 seconds to reheat. Serve at once.

## Two

1. Scrub the potatoes, prick the skins with a fork and place on a double thickness sheet of absorbent kitchen paper and microwave on HIGH for 10-12 minutes, turning over once, until tender and soft to the squeeze. Wrap in foil and leave to stand while preparing the filling.

2. Place the mushrooms in a bowl with the butter. Cover and microwave on HIGH for 1-1½ minutes, stirring once.

3. Thinly pare the rind from the brie and discard. Cut the brie into bite-sized cubes.

4. Unwrap the potatoes and cut each in half. Scoop out the cooked flesh into a bowl. Add the mushrooms and their juice, the brie, chives and salt and pepper to taste. Mix gently then return to their shells.

5. Place on a large serving plate and microwave on HIGH for 20-30 seconds to reheat.

VEGETARIAN MICROWAVE COOKING FOR ONE & TWO

# Mushroom and Pepper Fettucine

Garlic and herb-flavoured soft cheese makes an instant sauce for pasta. Here it is also combined with flavoursome brown cap mushrooms and peppers to make a wonderful lunch or supper dish.

| One | | Two |
|---|---|---|
| 75 g/3 oz | dried fettucine | 175 g/6 oz |
| 600 ml/1 pt | boiling water | 1.2 litres/2 pts |
| 7 g/¼ oz | butter or margarine | 15 g/½ oz |
| 1 | shallots, finely chopped | 2 |
| 25 g/1 oz | brown cap mushrooms, sliced | 50 g/2 oz |
| 1 | small red peppers, cored, seeded and sliced | 2 |
| 25 g/1 oz | garlic and herb-flavoured soft cheese | 50 g/2 oz |
| 30 ml/2 tbsp | single cream | 60 ml/4 tbsp |
| 15 ml/1 tbsp | milk | 30 ml/2 tbsp |
| | salt and pepper | |

## One

1. Place the pasta in a medium bowl and pour over the boiling water. Microwave on HIGH for 6-8 minutes, stirring once, halfway through the cooking time, until the pasta is just tender. Leave to stand while preparing the sauce.

2. Place the butter, shallot, mushrooms and pepper in a bowl. Cover and microwave on HIGH for 2 minutes, stirring once.

3. Add the soft cheese, cream, milk and salt and pepper to taste, mixing well. Microwave on HIGH for 30-45 seconds or until piping hot.

4. Drain the pasta thoroughly, add the sauce and toss well to combine. Serve at once.

## Two

1. Place the pasta in a large bowl and pour over the boiling water. Microwave on HIGH for 6-8 minutes, stirring once, halfway through the cooking time, until the pasta is just tender. Leave to stand while preparing the sauce.

2. Place the butter, shallots, mushrooms and pepper in a bowl. Cover and microwave on HIGH for 2½-3 minutes, stirring once.

3. Add the soft cheese, cream, milk and salt and pepper to taste, mixing well. Microwave on HIGH for about 1 minute or until piping hot.

4. Drain the pasta thoroughly, add the sauce and toss well to combine. Serve at once.

# THE MAIN EVENT

## Smoked Tofu in Mushroom Gravy

This is a very speedy main course dish using convenient vegetable gravy granules as the basis for the sauce. Mixed with mushrooms, Hoisin sauce, onion and smoked tofu the result is surprisingly tantalising.

| One | | Two |
| --- | --- | --- |
| 2.5 ml/½ tsp | vegetable oil | 5 ml/1 tsp |
| ½ | onion, peeled and finely sliced | 1 |
| 50 g/2 oz | mushrooms, sliced | 100 g/4 oz |
| 150 ml/¼ pt | vegetable gravy made with vegetable gravy granules (according to jar instructions) | 300 ml/½ pt |
| 15 ml/1 tbsp | Hoisin sauce | 30 ml/2 tbsp |
| 125 g/4 oz | smoked tofu, cubed or sliced | 225 g/8 oz |

### One

1. Place the oil and onion in a medium bowl, cover tightly and microwave on HIGH for 2 minutes, stirring once.

2. Stir in the mushrooms, re-cover and microwave on HIGH for 2 minutes, stirring once.

3. Add the vegetable gravy with the Hoisin sauce and the tofu, cover and microwave on HIGH for a further 1-2 minutes, stirring once, until heated through. Serve at once.

### Two

1. Place the oil and onion in a medium bowl, cover tightly and microwave on HIGH for 3 minutes, stirring once.

2. Stir in the mushrooms, re-cover and microwave on HIGH for 3 minutes, stirring once.

3. Add the vegetable gravy with the Hoisin sauce and the tofu, cover and microwave on HIGH for a further 2-3 minutes, stirring once, until heated through. Serve at once.

# Farmhouse Leek and Potato Bake

This recipe using potatoes, leeks, cheese and mushrooms makes a satisfying main course or hearty supper dish. Flash under a hot grill to give a crisp golden crust if you like.

| One | | Two |
|---|---|---|
| 250 g/9 oz | potatoes, peeled and cubed | 500 g/18 oz |
| 45 ml/3 tbsp | water | 90 ml/6 tbsp |
| 225 g/8 oz | leeks, thinly sliced | 450 g/1 lb |
| 50 g/2 oz | small button mushrooms, wiped | 100 g/4 oz |
| 1 | small bay leaf | 1 |
| 3 | black peppercorns | 3 |
| 125 ml/4 fl oz | milk | 250 ml/8 fl oz |
| 15 g/½ oz | butter or margarine | 25 g/1 oz |
| 15 g/½ oz | plain flour | 25 g/1 oz |
| 3.75 ml/¾ tsp | chopped mixed fresh herbs | 7.5 ml/1½ tsp |
| 40 g/1½ oz | vegetarian hard cheese, grated | 5 g/3 oz |
| | salt and pepper | |

## One

1. Place the potatoes in a bowl with half of the water. Cover and microwave on HIGH for about 4 minutes or until almost tender, stirring once halfway through the cooking time. Drain well.

2. Place the leeks in another bowl with the remaining water. Cover and microwave on HIGH for 3 minutes, stirring once halfway through cooking time. Drain reserving the cooking juices.

3. Place the mushrooms in a shallow dish with the bay leaf, peppercorns and one-third of the milk. Cover and microwave on HIGH for 45 seconds. Drain, reserving the cooking juices. Remove and discard the bay leaf and peppercorns.

4. Place the butter or margarine, flour, herbs and the remaining milk in a bowl and microwave on HIGH for 1-1½ minutes, whisking twice during the cooking time to keep the sauce smooth. Stir in the reserved cooking juices from the leeks and the mushrooms, one-third of the grated cheese and salt and pepper to taste, mixing well.

5. Mix the leeks and mushrooms together and place in a shallow dish. Pour over the sauce then top with the potatoes. Sprinkle with the remaining cheese and microwave on HIGH for 1-1½ minutes until the vegetables are tender and the cheese has melted. Flash under a hot grill to brown if you like before serving.

## Two

1. Place the potatoes in a bowl with half of the water. Cover and microwave on HIGH for about 8 minutes or until almost tender, stirring once halfway through the cooking time. Drain well.

2. Place the leeks in another bowl with the remaining water. Cover and microwave on HIGH for 5-6 minutes, stirring once halfway through the cooking time. Drain reserving the cooking juices.

3. Place the mushrooms in a shallow dish with the bay leaf, peppercorns and one-third of the milk. Cover and microwave on HIGH for 1½ minutes. Drain, reserving the cooking juices. Remove and discard the bay leaf and peppercorns.

4. Place the butter or margarine, flour, herbs and the remaining milk in a bowl and microwave on HIGH for 2 minutes, whisking twice during the cooking time to keep the sauce smooth. Stir in the reserved cooking juices from the leeks and the mushrooms, one-third of the grated cheese and salt and pepper to taste, mixing well.

5. Mix the leeks and mushrooms together and place in a shallow dish. Pour over the sauce then top with the potatoes. Sprinkle with the remaining cheese and microwave on HIGH for 2 minutes until the vegetables are tender and the cheese has melted. Flash under a hot grill to brown if you like before serving.

# Summer Vegetable Bonanza

Here is a tasty dish of freshly cooked tagliatelle tossed with summer green vegetables in a delicious creamy sauce. For speed use fresh tagliatelle but if dried is your only option then increase the pasta cooking time to 6 minutes.

| One | | Two |
|---|---|---|
| 15 g/½ oz | butter | 25 g/1 oz |
| ¼ | onion, peeled and finely chopped | ½ |
| 75 g/3 oz | frozen broad beans, thawed | 175 g/6 oz |
| 25 g/1 oz | frozen petits pois, thawed | 50 g/2 oz |
| 40 g/1½ oz | chicory, finely sliced | 75 g/3 oz |
| 10 ml/2 tsp | fresh chopped parsley | 20 ml/4 tsp |
| 75 ml/5 tbsp | extra thick double cream | 150 ml/¼ pt |
| 15 ml/1 tbsp | freshly grated vegetarian Parmesan cheese | 30 ml/2 tbsp |
| | salt and pepper | |
| 100 g/4 oz | fresh white and green tagliatelle | 225 g/8 oz |
| 350 ml/12 fl oz | boiling water | 750 ml/1 ¼ pt |
| 15 ml/1 tbsp | shaved vegetarian Parmesan cheese | 30 ml/2 tbsp |
| | flat-leaf parsley sprigs, to garnish | |

## One

1. Place the butter in a medium bowl with the onion, cover and microwave on HIGH for 1 minute.

2. Add the broad beans and petits pois, mixing well. Cover and microwave on HIGH for 1-1½ minutes, stirring once.

3. Add the chicory and parsley, re-cover and microwave on HIGH for a further 1 minute.

4. Stir in the cream, grated Parmesan and salt and pepper to taste, blending well. Re-cover and microwave on HIGH for 1 minute, stirring once until the vegetables are tender and the sauce is hot and bubbly. Leave to stand, covered, while cooking the pasta.

5. Place the pasta in a medium bowl and pour over the boiling water. Microwave on HIGH for 2-3 minutes. Drain thoroughly and transfer to a warmed serving dish. Add the vegetable mixture with the sauce and toss gently to mix.

6. Sprinkle with the shaved Parmesan, garnish with the flat-leaf parsley and serve at once.

## Two

1. Place the butter in a medium bowl with the onion, cover and microwave on HIGH for 1¼ minutes.

2. Add the broad beans and petits pois, mixing well. Cover and microwave on HIGH for 1½-2 minutes, stirring once.

3. Add the chicory and parsley, re-cover and microwave on HIGH for a further 1½ minutes.

4. Stir in the cream, grated Parmesan and salt and pepper to taste, blending well. Re-cover and microwave on HIGH for 1½ minutes, stirring once until the vegetables are tender and the sauce is hot and bubbly. Leave to stand, covered, while cooking the pasta.

5. Place the pasta in a medium bowl and pour over the boiling water. Microwave on HIGH for 2-3 minutes. Drain thoroughly and transfer to a warmed serving dish. Add the vegetable mixture with the sauce and toss gently to mix.

6. Sprinkle with the shaved Parmesan, garnish with the flat-leaf parsley and serve at once.

# Vegetable and Macaroni Cheese

Here is a hearty pasta and vegetable dish to ring the changes to the more familiar macaroni cheese. Serve with a crisp coleslaw salad.

| One | | Two |
|---|---|---|
| 50 g/2 oz | macaroni | 100 g/4 oz |
| 2.5 ml/½ tsp | oil | 5 ml/1 tsp |
| 300 ml/½ pt | boiling water | 600 ml/1 pt |
| 20 g/¾ oz | butter or margarine | 40 g/1½ oz |
| ¼ | large onion, peeled and sliced | ½ |
| ½ | small clove of garlic, crushed | 1 |
| 50 g/2 oz | sliced or chopped | 100 g/4 oz |
| | mixed vegetables (carrot, courgette, peas, sweetcorn and green beans, for example) | |
| | salt and pepper | |
| 15 g/½ oz | plain flour | 25 g/1 oz |
| 125 ml/4 fl oz | milk | 225 ml/7½ fl oz |
| 25 g/1 oz | vegetarian Cheddar cheese, grated | 50 g/2 oz |
| 10 ml/2 tsp | single cream or natural fromage frais | 20 ml/4 tsp |

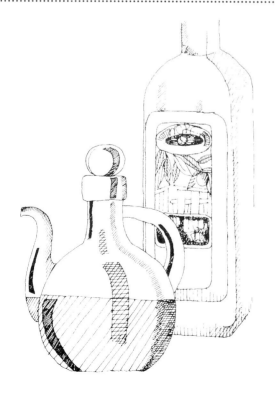

## One

1. Place the pasta in a medium bowl with the oil and boiling water. Microwave on HIGH for 10 minutes, stirring once. Leave to stand for 3-5 minutes, then drain thoroughly.

2. Meanwhile, place one-third of the butter in a small serving dish and microwave on HIGH for 15-30 seconds to melt. Add the onion and garlic and microwave on HIGH for 1 minute.

3. Add the prepared vegetables, mixing well, cover and microwave on HIGH for 2-3 minutes, until tender crisp.

4. Add the pasta to the vegetables with salt and pepper to taste.

5. Place the remaining butter in a small bowl and microwave on HIGH for about 30 seconds to melt. Add the flour and mix well, then gradually add the milk. Microwave on HIGH for 2-2½ minutes, beating every 1 minute until smooth and thickened. Add most of the cheese and the cream or fromage frais, mixing well.

6. Mix the prepared sauce with the pasta and vegetable mixture, then sprinkle with the remaining cheese. Either microwave on HIGH for 1-2 minutes until the cheese melts or brown under a preheated hot grill until golden and bubbly. Serve hot.

## Two

1. Place the pasta in a medium bowl with the oil and boiling water. Microwave on HIGH for 10 minutes, stirring once. Leave to stand for 3-5 minutes, then drain thoroughly.

2. Meanwhile, place one-third of the butter in a medium serving dish and microwave on HIGH for about 1 minute to melt. Add the onion and garlic and microwave on HIGH for 1½-2 minutes.

3. Add the prepared vegetables, mixing well. Cover and microwave on HIGH for 4-4½ minutes, until tender crisp.

4. Add the pasta to the vegetables with salt and pepper to taste.

5. Place the remaining butter in a medium bowl and microwave on HIGH for about 45-60 seconds to melt. Add the flour and mix well, then gradually add the milk. Microwave on HIGH for 4-5 minutes, beating every 1 minute until smooth and thickened. Add most of the cheese and the cream or fromage frais, mixing well.

6. Mix the prepared sauce with the pasta and vegetable mixture, then sprinkle with the remaining cheese. Either microwave on HIGH for about 2 minutes until the cheese melts or brown under a preheated hot grill until golden and bubbly. Serve hot.

## *Wholewheat Pasta with Spicy Peanut and Cucumber Sauce*

This is a delicious and simple way to enjoy Thai flavours with little culinary effort and precious time.

| One | | Two |
|---|---|---|
| 40 g/1½ oz | creamy peanut butter | 75 g/3 oz |
| 5-10 ml/1-2 tsp | soy sauce | 10-20 ml/2-4 tsp |
| 5-10 ml/1-2 tsp | lime juice | 10-20 ml/2-4 tsp |
| ¼ | clove of garlic, crushed | ½ |
| | pinch of dried red pepper flakes | |
| | pinch of sugar | |
| 30 ml/2 tbsp | hot water | 60 ml/4 tbsp |
| 100 g/4 oz | dried wholewheat pasta | 225 g/8 oz |
| 600 ml/1 pt | boiling water | 1.2 litres/2 pts |
| ¼ | cucumber, peeled, seeded and cut diagonally into slices | ½ |
| 2 | spring onions, finely sliced | 4 |
| ¼ | red pepper, cored, seeded and sliced | ½ |
| | salt and pepper | |

## One and Two

1. Place the peanut butter, soy sauce, lime juice, garlic, red pepper flakes, sugar and hot water in a blender or food processor and process until smooth.

2. Place the pasta in a medium bowl and cover with the boiling water. Microwave on HIGH for 10-12 minutes, stirring once until the pasta is cooked al dente. Leave to stand for 2 minutes, then drain thoroughly. Rinse briefly under cold running water and drain well.

3. In a medium serving bowl, toss the cooked and cooled pasta with the peanut sauce, cucumber, spring onions, red pepper and salt and pepper to taste, blending well. Serve at once.

## *Three Cheese Pasta with Walnuts*

This pasta dish is best made with fresh pasta since it seems to soak up the deliciously cheesy sauce better than dried. The walnuts give added crunch and nutrition.

| One | | Two |
|---|---|---|
| 100 g/4 oz | fresh ribbon pasta | 225 g/8 oz |
| 375 ml/13 fl oz | boiling water | 750 ml/1¼ pts |
| 25 g/1 oz | vegetarian hard blue cheese | 50 g/2 oz |
| 15 g/½ oz | freshly grated vegetarian Parmesan cheese | 25 g/1 oz |
| 25 g/1 oz | mascarpone cheese | 50 g/2 oz |
| 37.5 ml/2½ tbsp | double cream | 75 ml/5 tbsp |
| 25 g/1 oz | shelled walnuts, coarsely broken into pieces | 50 g/2 oz |
| | salt and pepper | |

## One

1. Place the pasta in a large dish and pour over the boiling water. Cover and microwave on HIGH for 2-3 minutes. Leave to stand while preparing the sauce.

2. Crumble the blue cheese into a bowl, add the Parmesan, mascarpone and cream. Microwave on HIGH for 1-1½ minutes, stirring twice, until the sauce is melted and smooth. Stir in the walnut pieces and season to taste with salt and pepper.

3. Drain the pasta thoroughly and add to the sauce mixture. Toss well to coat in the cheesy sauce. Serve at once.

## Two

1. Place the pasta in a large dish and pour over the boiling water. Cover and microwave on HIGH for 2-3 minutes. Leave to stand while preparing the sauce.

2. Crumble the blue cheese into a bowl, add the Parmesan, mascarpone and cream. Microwave on HIGH for 1½-2 minutes, stirring twice, until the sauce is melted and smooth. Stir in the walnut pieces and season to taste with salt and pepper.

3. Drain the pasta thoroughly and add to the sauce mixture. Toss well to coat in the cheesy sauce. Serve at once.

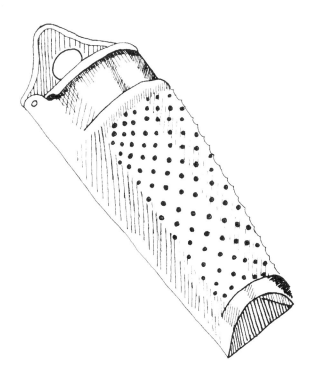

# *Falafels*

Falafels are delicious chick-pea rissoles that are Middle Eastern in origin. They are delicious served as a snack in pockets of pitta bread, topped with chopped tomatoes, lettuce, spring onion and natural yogurt but can be served as a main meal with a salad of the same ingredients and fingers of pitta bread. You will need a browning dish to prepare this recipe.

| One | | Two |
|---|---|---|
| ½ | 432 g/15 oz can chick peas, drained and rinsed | 1 |
| 25 g/1 oz | bulghur or cracked wheat, soaked in cold water for 1 hour, then squeezed very dry | 50 g/2 oz |
| 1 | cloves of garlic, peeled and crushed | 2 |
| 7.5 ml/1½ tsp | plain flour | 15 ml/1 tbsp |
| ½ | egg, beaten | 1 |
| 1.25 ml/¼ tsp | ground coriander | 2.5 ml/½ tsp |
| 1.25 ml/¼ tsp | ground cumin | 2.5 ml/½ tsp |
| | pinch of ground turmeric | |
| | pinch of mild chilli powder | |
| 7.5 ml/1½ tsp | chopped fresh parsley | 15 ml/1 tbsp |
| 7.5 ml/1½ tsp | tahini | 15 ml/1 tbsp |
| | salt and pepper | |
| | paprika, for sprinkling | |
| | vegetable oil, for brushing | |

## One

1. Purée the chick peas in a blender or mash very finely with a fork. Add the bulghur, garlic, flour, egg, spices, parsley, tahini and salt and pepper to taste, mixing very well. Chill thoroughly until the mixture is firm enough to shape.

2. Divide and shape the mixture into about 10 small balls about the size of walnuts and sprinkle with paprika to dust lightly.

3. Preheat a browning dish according to the manufacturer's instructions, add the oil and brush to coat the base lightly. Add the falafels in a circle in the dish, pressing down lightly so that the underside

browns and microwave on HIGH for 5 minutes, or until cooked, turning over once halfway through the cooking time to brown on all sides. Serve hot or allow to cool and serve cold.

## Two

1. Purée the chick peas in a blender or mash very finely with a fork. Add the bulghur, garlic, flour, egg, spices, parsley, tahini and salt and pepper to taste, mixing very well. Chill thoroughly until the mixture is firm enough to shape.

2. Divide and shape the mixture into about 20 small balls about the size of walnuts and sprinkle with paprika to dust lightly.

3. Preheat a browning dish according to the manufacturer's instructions, add the oil and brush to coat the base lightly. Add half of the falafels in a circle in the dish, pressing down lightly so that the underside browns and microwave on HIGH for 5 minutes, or until cooked, turning over once halfway through the cooking time to brown on all sides. Remove to a serving dish and keep warm. Preheat the browning dish again and cook the remaining falafels as above. Serve hot or allow to cool and serve cold.

# Vegetable and Bean Ragoût

A very satisfying dish of mixed vegetables in a well-flavoured sauce. Serve with couscous or rice.

| One | | Two |
| --- | --- | --- |
| ¼ | large onion, peeled and chopped | ½ |
| ½ | carrot, peeled and thinly sliced | 1 |
| ½ | small parsnip, thinly sliced | 1 |
| ½ | potato, cubed | 1 |
| 37.5 ml/2½ tbsp | water | 75 ml/5 tbsp |
| 100 g/4 oz | baked beans in tomato sauce | 225 g/8 oz |
| 100 g/4 oz | canned chopped tomatoes | 225 g/8 oz |
| 1.25 ml/¼ tsp | dried mint | 2.5 ml/½ tsp |
| 7.5 ml/1½ tsp | vegetable gravy granules | 15 ml/1 tbsp |

## One

1. Place the onion, carrot, parsnip and potato in a medium bowl with the water. Cover and microwave on HIGH for 4-5 minutes, stirring once until softened.

2. Stir in the beans, tomatoes and mint. Sprinkle the vegetable gravy granules over the top and stir in. Cover and microwave on HIGH for 1-2 minutes, stirring once.

3. Serve hot with rice or couscous.

## Two

1. Place the onion, carrot, parsnip and potato in a medium bowl with the water. Cover and microwave on HIGH for 8-10 minutes, stirring once until softened.

2. Stir in the beans, tomatoes and mint. Sprinkle the vegetable gravy granules over the top and stir in. Cover and microwave on HIGH for 1½-2½ minutes, stirring once.

3. Serve hot with rice or couscous.

# Rice Against Time

This is a recipe for a nutty peanut and beanshoot risotto flavoured with mushrooms, tamari or soy sauce and coriander. The dish can be substantially speeded up if you use cooked rice (if so, simply omit stage 1).

| One | | Two |
|---|---|---|
| 50 g/2 oz | long-grain brown rice | 100 g/4 oz |
| 150 ml/¼ pt | boiling vegetable stock | 300 ml/½ pt |
| 5 ml/1 tsp | vegetable oil | 10 ml/2 tsp |
| ½ | medium onion, peeled and chopped | 1 |
| 25 g/1 oz | mushrooms, wiped and sliced | 50 g/2 oz |
| 3.75 ml/¾ tsp | tamari or soy sauce | 7.5 ml/1½ tsp |
| | salt and pepper | |
| 15 g/½ oz | peanuts | 25 g/1 oz |
| 40 g/1½ oz | beanshoots | 75 g/3 oz |
| ½ | avocado, peeled, stoned and sliced | 1 |
| 5 ml/1 tsp | lemon juice | 10 ml/2 tsp |

## One

1. Place the rice in a small bowl and add the boiling stock. Cover and microwave on HIGH for 3 minutes. Reduce the power setting to MEDIUM and microwave for a further 20-25 minutes, stirring 2-3 times, or until the rice is cooked. Drain if necessary.

2. Place the oil and onion in a medium dish, cover and microwave on HIGH for 1 minute. Add the cooked rice, mushrooms, tamari or soy sauce and salt and pepper to taste. Cover and microwave on HIGH for 1-1½ minutes, stirring once.

3. Add the peanuts and beanshoots to the risotto, mixing well. Microwave, uncovered, for 1-1½ minutes, until the mixture is heated through, stirring twice.

4. Meanwhile, toss the avocado in the lemon juice. Add to the hot risotto, leave to stand, covered, for 1-2 minutes to warm the avocado, then serve at once.

## Two

1. Place the rice in a medium bowl and add the boiling stock. Cover and microwave on HIGH for 3 minutes. Reduce the power setting to MEDIUM and microwave for a further 20-25 minutes, stirring 2-3 times, or until the rice is cooked. Drain if necessary.

2. Place the oil and onion in a medium dish, cover and microwave on HIGH for 2 minutes. Add the cooked rice, mushrooms, tamari or soy sauce and salt and pepper to taste. Cover and microwave on HIGH for 2-3 minutes, stirring once.

3. Add the peanuts and beanshoots to the risotto, mixing well. Microwave, uncovered, for 2-3 minutes, until the mixture is heated through, stirring twice.

4. Meanwhile, toss the avocado in the lemon juice. Add to the hot risotto, leave to stand, covered, for 1-2 minutes to warm the avocado, then serve at once.

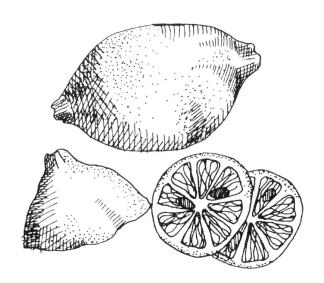

# Spaghetti Squash with Tomato and Dill Sauce

Squashes are amazingly versatile and are superbly suited to microwave cooking. This recipe uses spaghetti squash, a rugby ball shaped squash with thick skin but wonderfully sweet flesh. Here it is cooked until tender then forked out on to a dish and topped with a savoury tomato and dill sauce.

| One | | Two |
| --- | --- | --- |
| ½ | spaghetti squash, weighing about 450 g/1 lb | 1 |
| 15 ml/1 tbsp | water | 30 ml/2 tbsp |
| 7.5 ml/1½ tsp | olive oil | 15 ml/1 tbsp |
| 1 | shallots, peeled and finely chopped | 2 |
| ½ | clove of garlic, crushed | 1 |
| 3 | ripe plum tomatoes, peeled, seeded and coarsely chopped | 6 |
| | salt and pepper | |
| 7.5 ml/1½ tsp | chopped fresh dill | 15 ml/1 tbsp |
| | shaved vegetarian Parmesan cheese, to serve | |

## One

1. Deseed the halved squash and remove any fibres. Place cut side down in a shallow dish with the water. Cover loosely and microwave on HIGH for 10-14 minutes, until tender.

2. Place the oil in a bowl with the shallot and garlic. Cover and microwave on HIGH for 30 seconds. Add the tomatoes and salt and pepper to taste, mixing well. Microwave on HIGH for about 3 minutes, stirring once. Stir in the dill.

3. Drain the squash and fork out the flesh into a warmed serving dish. Spoon the cooked tomato and dill sauce over the top and scatter with shaved Parmesan cheese to serve.

## Two

1. Halve the squash. Deseed the halved squashes and remove any fibres. Place the two halves, cut side down, in a large shallow dish with the water. Cover loosely and microwave on HIGH for 15-20 minutes, turning and re-arranging once halfway through the cooking time, until tender.

2. Place the oil in a bowl with the shallots and garlic. Cover and microwave on HIGH for 45 seconds. Add the tomatoes and salt and pepper to taste, mixing well. Microwave on HIGH for about 4½ minutes, stirring once. Stir in the dill.

3. Drain the squash and fork out the flesh into a warmed serving dish. Spoon the cooked tomato and dill sauce over the top and scatter with shaved Parmesan cheese to serve.

# Summer-Style Pasta with Beans

This is a hearty cold pasta and bean dish ideal to serve when appetites are large after summer time swimming, tennis or other outdoor activities.

| One | | Two |
|---|---|---|
| 75 g/3 oz | dried penne | 175 g/6 oz |
| 600 ml/1 pt | boiling water | 1.2 litres/2 pts |
| ½ | 400 g/14 oz can cannellini beans, rinsed and drained | 1 |
| 1 | large plum tomatoes, coarsely chopped | 2 |
| 15 ml/1 tbsp | chopped fresh basil | 30 ml/2 tbsp |
| 10 ml/2 tsp | capers | 20 ml/4 tsp |
| 15 ml/1 tbsp | extra-virgin olive oil | 30 ml/2 tbsp |
| 5 ml/1 tsp | white wine vinegar | 10 ml/2 tsp |
| | salt and pepper | |
| 50 g/2 oz | vegetarian cheese, cut into matchsticks | 100 g/4 oz |

## One and Two

1. Place the pasta in a large bowl and pour over the boiling water. Microwave on HIGH for 10-12 minutes, stirring once halfway through the cooking time, until the pasta is just tender. Leave to stand for 3 minutes before draining thoroughly. Allow to cool.

2. Meanwhile, mix the beans with the tomato, basil and capers.

3. Add the cooled pasta to the bean mixture and toss gently to mix.

4. Beat the oil with the wine vinegar and salt and pepper to taste. Drizzle over the pasta and bean mixture and toss gently to mix.

5. To serve, spoon the pasta and bean mixture on to one or two individual serving plates and scatter over the cheese. Serve as soon as possible.

# Penne Arrabbiata

If you love pasta with regional sauces then this is the recipe for you - penne, or pasta quills, cooked and served with a southern Italian sauce made from tomatoes, garlic, onions and chillies. Serve sprinkled with grated vegetarian Parmesan.

| One | | Two |
|---|---|---|
| 7.5 ml/1½ tsp | olive oil | 15 ml/1 tbsp |
| ¼ | onion, peeled and finely chopped | ½ |
| ½ | clove of garlic, crushed | 1 |
| ½ | chilli, finely chopped | 1 |
| ½ | 200 g/7 oz can chopped tomatoes | 1 |
| 7.5 ml/1½ tsp | tomato purée | 15 ml/1 tbsp |
| | salt and pepper | |
| 75 g/3 oz | dried penne | 175 g/6 oz |
| 600 ml/1 pt | boiling water | 1.2 litres/2 pts |
| | grated vegetarian Parmesan, to serve | |

## One

1. Place the oil in a medium bowl with the onion, garlic and chilli. Cover tightly and microwave on HIGH for 1 minute until softened.

2. Add the tomatoes, tomato purée and salt and pepper to taste, blending well. Cover tightly and microwave on HIGH for 3-4 minutes, stirring twice, until hot, bubbly and well blended. Leave to stand, covered, while cooking the pasta.

3. Place the pasta in a medium bowl and cover with the boiling water. Microwave on HIGH for 10-12 minutes, stirring once halfway through the cooking time, until the pasta is just tender. Allow to stand for 2 minutes, then drain thoroughly.

4. Add the cooked sauce to the pasta and toss gently to mix. Spoon on to a warmed serving plate and sprinkle with grated Parmesan to serve.

## Two

1. Place the oil in a medium bowl with the onion, garlic and chilli. Cover tightly and microwave on HIGH for 1½ minutes until softened.

2. Add the tomatoes, tomato purée and salt and pepper to taste, blending well. Cover tightly and microwave on HIGH for 5-6 minutes, stirring twice, until hot, bubbly and well blended. Leave to stand, covered, while cooking the pasta.

3. Place the pasta in a large bowl and cover with the boiling water. Microwave on HIGH for 10-12 minutes, stirring once halfway through the cooking time, until the pasta is just tender. Allow to stand for 2 minutes, then drain thoroughly.

4. Add the cooked sauce to the pasta and toss gently to mix. Spoon on to two warmed serving plates and sprinkle with grated Parmesan to serve.

# Quorn Bolognese

Quorn is a myco-protein that is vegetable in origin, low in fat, contains no cholesterol and yet has as much protein as an egg. It comes either as tender pieces or as a versatile mince. Use the latter to make this tasty bolognese for serving with pasta.

| One | | Two |
| --- | --- | --- |
| 7.5 ml/1½ tsp | olive oil | 15 ml/1 tbsp |
| ¼ | large onion, peeled and chopped | ½ |
| ½ | clove of garlic, crushed | 1 |
| 75 g/3 oz | minced Quorn | 175 g/6 oz |
| 1.25 ml/¼ tsp | dried mixed herbs | 2.5 ml/½ tsp |
| 2.5 ml/½ tsp | red pesto | 5 ml/1 tsp |
| 7.5 ml/1½ tsp | tomato purée | 15 ml/1 tbsp |
| 100 g/4 oz | canned chopped tomatoes | 225 g/8 oz |
| 30 ml/2 tbsp | red wine | 60 ml/4 tbsp |
| 2.5 ml/½ tsp | sugar | 5 ml/1 tsp |
| | salt and pepper | |

## One

1. Place the oil in a medium bowl with the onion and garlic. Cover and microwave on HIGH for 1 minute.

2. Add the Quorn and dried herbs and microwave on HIGH for 1½-2 minutes, stirring once.

3. Add the red pesto, tomato purée, chopped tomatoes, wine, sugar and salt and pepper to taste, blending well. Partially-cover and microwave on HIGH for 5-6 minutes, or until the mixture is thick and pulpy, stirring twice.

4. Serve hot with cooked pasta and a seasonal salad.

## Two

1. Place the oil in a large bowl with the onion and garlic. Cover and microwave on HIGH for 1½ minutes.

2. Add the Quorn and dried herbs and microwave on HIGH for 2-3 minutes, stirring once.

3. Add the red pesto, tomato purée, chopped tomatoes, wine, sugar and salt and pepper to taste, blending well. Partially-cover and microwave on HIGH for 7-9 minutes, or until the sauce is thick and pulpy, stirring twice.

4. Serve hot with cooked pasta and a seasonal salad.

# Lentil 'Bolognese' Sauce for Spaghetti

This is the nearest thing to the traditional meat sauce that accompanies spaghetti. It is just the dish to serve to meat-eating vegetarian sceptics - I doubt if they will notice the difference! You can use the same mixture to layer sheets of pasta with a cheesy sauce to make a lasagne or add a little chilli powder and cooked red kidney beans to make a chilli.

| One | | Two |
|---|---|---|
| 10 ml/2 tsp | olive oil | 20 ml/4 tsp |
| 1 | onions, peeled and chopped | 2 |
| ½ | clove of garlic, crushed | 1 |
| 1 | sticks of celery, finely chopped | 2 |
| 1 | carrots, peeled and finely chopped | 2 |
| ½ | 440 g/15¾ oz can brown lentils in water, salt and spice | 1 |
| 7.5 ml/1½ tsp | tomato purée | 15 ml/1 tbsp |
| 50 g/2 oz | mushrooms, wiped and sliced | 100 g/4 oz |
| ½ | small cooking apple, peeled, cored and grated | 1 |
| 50 ml/2 fl oz | cider or water | 100 ml/4 fl oz |
| ½ | vegetable stock cube | 1 |
| | salt and pepper | |
| 15 ml/1 tbsp | chopped parsley | 30 ml/2 tbsp |

## One

1. Place the oil, onion, garlic, celery and carrots in a large bowl. Cover and microwave on HIGH for 4-5 minutes, stirring once, until softened.

2. Drain the lentils thoroughly and add to the vegetables with the tomato purée, mushrooms, apple, cider or water, crumbled stock cube and salt and pepper to taste, mixing very well to combine. Cover and microwave on HIGH for 5-6 minutes, stirring once.

3. Stir in the parsley and leave to stand, covered, while cooking the pasta accompaniment. Stir well before serving.

## Two

1. Place the oil, onion, garlic, celery and carrots in a large bowl. Cover and microwave on HIGH for 6-8 minutes, stirring once, until softened.

2. Drain the lentils thoroughly and add to the vegetables with the tomato purée, mushrooms, apple, cider or water, crumbled stock cube and salt and pepper to taste, mixing very well to combine. Cover and microwave on HIGH for 7-9 minutes, stirring once.

3. Stir in the parsley and leave to stand, covered, while cooking the pasta accompaniment. Stir well before serving.

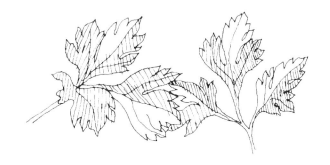

# Midwinter Root Pie

This is a sort of cheese and potato pie with added vegetables. It is just the kind of hearty and warming fare needed in the depths of mid-winter. Portion sizes in this recipe are large - certainly ample to satisfy man-sized appetites.

| One | | Two |
| --- | --- | --- |
| 450 g/1 lb | potatoes, peeled and cut into small, even-sized pieces | 900 g/2 lb |
| 175 g/6 oz | swede, peeled and cut into small chunks | 350 g/12 oz |
| 100 g/4 oz | carrots, peeled and sliced | 225 g/8 oz |
| 75 ml/5 tbsp | water | 150 ml/¼ pt |
| 15 g/½ oz | butter | 25 g/1 oz |
| ½ | onion, peeled and sliced | 1 |
| 50 ml/2 fl oz | milk | 100 ml/4 fl oz |
| | pinch of grated nutmeg | |
| | salt and pepper | |
| 75 g/3 oz | vegetarian hard cheese, grated | 175 g/6 oz |
| | tomato slices and parsley sprigs, to garnish | |

## One

1. Place the potatoes, swede and carrots in a large bowl with the water. Cover and microwave on HIGH for 12-14 minutes, stirring twice, until tender. Drain thoroughly.

2. Place the butter in a bowl with the onion. Cover and microwave on HIGH for 2 minutes, stirring once.

3. Place the milk in a small jug and microwave on HIGH for 45-60 seconds to warm.

4. Add the milk, nutmeg and salt and pepper to taste to the drained vegetables and mash until smooth and well blended. Stir in the onion mixture and most of the cheese.

5. Turn the mixture into a flameproof dish and sprinkle with the remaining cheese. Top with tomato slices to garnish then cook under a preheated hot grill until the cheese has melted and starts to bubble. Alternatively, return to the microwave and cook on HIGH for a further 2-3 minutes until heated through. Garnish with parsley sprigs and serve at once.

## Two

1. Place the potatoes, swede and carrots in a large bowl with the water. Cover and microwave on HIGH for 20-25 minutes, stirring twice, until tender. Drain thoroughly.

2. Place the butter in a bowl with the onion. Cover and microwave on HIGH for 3½ minutes, stirring once.

3. Place the milk in a small jug and microwave on HIGH for 1½ minutes to warm.

4. Add the milk, nutmeg and salt and pepper to taste to the drained vegetables and mash until smooth and well blended. Stir in the onion mixture and most of the cheese.

5. Turn the mixture into one large or two individual flameproof dishes and sprinkle with the remaining cheese. Top with tomato slices to garnish then cook under a preheated hot grill until the cheese has melted and starts to bubble. Alternatively, return to the microwave and cook on HIGH for a further 3-3½ minutes until heated through. Garnish with parsley sprigs and serve at once.

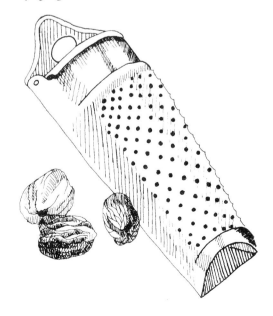

# ONE POT SPECIALS

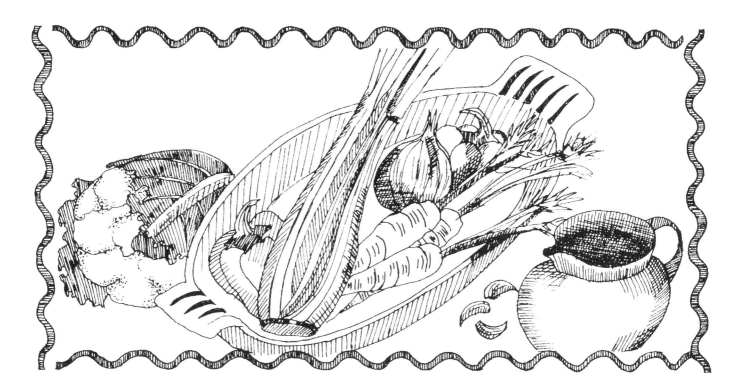

## *Senorita's Barley*

This one-pot main course dish of barley is cooked with an array of typically Spanish ingredients - onions, tomatoes, peppers and olives. Try adding a little cubed vegetarian hard cheese just before serving.

| One | | Two |
|---|---|---|
| 75 g/3 oz | barley | 175 g/6 oz |
| 500 ml/17 fl oz | boiling water or vegetable stock | 1 litre/1¾ pts |
| 5 ml/1 tsp | olive oil | 10 ml/2 tsp |
| ¼ | Spanish onion, chopped | ½ |
| ½ | clove of garlic, crushed | 1 |
| ¼ | small green pepper, cored, seeded and chopped | ½ |
| pinch | ground paprika | 1.25 ml/¼ tsp |
| 50 g/2 oz | chopped canned tomatoes | 100 g/4 oz |
| | salt and pepper | |
| 2-3 | black olives, stoned and sliced | 4-6 |

## One

1. Place the barley in a medium dish with the boiling water or stock. Cover loosely and microwave on HIGH for 3 minutes. Reduce the power setting to MEDIUM and microwave for 25 minutes, stirring three times. Leave to stand, covered, for 5 minutes, then drain thoroughly.

2. Meanwhile, place the oil, onion, garlic and green pepper in a bowl, cover and microwave on HIGH for 1½-2 minutes, until softened.

3. Stir in the paprika and microwave on HIGH for a further 30 seconds.

4. Stir in the cooked barley, tomatoes and salt and pepper to taste, mixing well. Microwave on MEDIUM for about 3-5 minutes, or until most of the tomato juices have been absorbed by the barley.

5. Stir in the black olives and serve while still hot.

## Two

1. Place the barley in a large dish with the boiling water or stock. Cover loosely and microwave on HIGH for 3 minutes. Reduce the power setting to MEDIUM and microwave for 25 minutes, stirring three times. Leave to stand, covered, for 5 minutes, then drain thoroughly.

2. Meanwhile, place the oil, onion, garlic and green pepper in a bowl and microwave on HIGH for 2-3 minutes, until softened.

3. Stir in the paprika and microwave on HIGH for a further 45 seconds.

4. Stir in the cooked barley, tomatoes and salt and pepper to taste, mixing well. Microwave on MEDIUM for about 4-6 minutes, or until most of the tomato juices have been absorbed by the barley.

5. Stir in the black olives and serve while still hot.

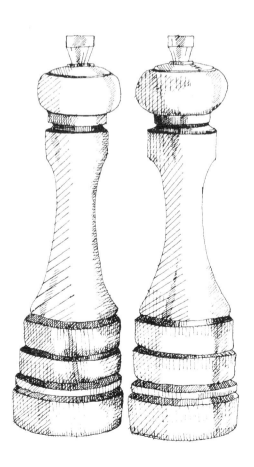

# Cowboy Blackeye Beans

I don't know if cowboys eat blackeye beans but I do know that this bean recipe has flavours similar to firepot baked beans of cowboy origin. The recipe isn't necessarily a speedy one and does require a little pre-soaking of the beans but once in the pot it doesn't need much further attention. Serve with crusty bread or jacket-baked potatoes if you like.

| One | | Two |
|---|---|---|
| 40 g/1½ oz | dried blackeye beans, soaked overnight in cold water | 75 g/3 oz |
| 600 ml/1 pt | boiling water | 900 ml/1½ pts |
| ½ | small onion, peeled and chopped | 1 |
| ½ | clove of garlic, crushed | 1 |
| 75 ml/5 tbsp | passata (Italian creamed tomatoes) | 150 ml/¼ pt |
| ½ | 200 g/7 oz can chopped tomatoes with herbs or chilli seasoning | 1 |
| 15 ml/1 tbsp | white wine vinegar | 30 ml/2 tbsp |
| 7.5 ml/1½ tsp | brown sugar | 15 ml/1 tbsp |
| 7.5 ml/1½ tsp | treacle or molasses | 15 ml/1 tbsp |
| 100 ml/3½ fl oz | cider or apple juice | 200 ml/7 fl oz |
| | salt and pepper | |
| | natural thickened yogurt or soured cream to serve (*optional*) | |
| | chopped parsley, to garnish | |

## One

1. Rinse and drain the beans from their soaking liquid and place in a large bowl with the boiling water. Cover and microwave on HIGH for about 12-13 minutes, during which time the beans should have been boiling for 10 minutes. If they have not boiled for 10 minutes, then microwave on HIGH until this time has been completed.

2. Drain the beans thoroughly and return to the bowl. Add all the remaining ingredients with salt and pepper to taste, mixing well. Cover and microwave on MEDIUM for 25-35 minutes, stirring 3 times during the cooking time, until the beans are tender

and the sauce is thick, bubbly and syrupy. If the mixture starts to cook a little too dry before the beans are tender, then add a little more cider or apple juice.

3. Leave to stand, covered, for 5 minutes before serving with crusty bread or jacket-baked potatoes. Top with a spoonful of natural thickened yogurt or soured cream if you like before serving and garnish with a sprinkling of chopped parsley.

## Two

1. Rinse and drain the beans from their soaking liquid and place in a large bowl with the boiling water. Cover and microwave on HIGH for 15-16 minutes, during which time the beans should have been boiling for 10 minutes. If they have not boiled for 10 minutes, then microwave on HIGH until this time has been completed.

2. Drain the beans thoroughly and return to the bowl. Add all the remaining ingredients with salt and pepper to taste, mixing well. Cover and microwave on MEDIUM for 35-40 minutes, stirring 3 times during the cooking time, until the beans are tender and the sauce is thick, bubbly and syrupy. If the mixture starts to cook a little too dry before the beans are tender, then add a little more cider or apple juice.

3. Leave to stand, covered, for 5 minutes before serving with crusty bread or jacket-baked potatoes. Top with a spoonful of natural thickened yogurt or soured cream if you like before serving and garnish with a sprinkling of chopped parsley.

# Spicy Vegetable Couscous

This is a tasty and colourful dish of peppers, carrot, red onion and celery cooked in a most flavoursome sauce, then mixed with couscous to make a fine one-pot meal. Serve with a small bowl of ready-made harissa if you like it hot.

| One | | Two |
|---|---|---|
| 30 ml/2 tbsp | olive oil | 60 ml/4 tbsp |
| ¼ | stick of celery, chopped | ½ |
| ¼ | red pepper, cored, seeded and chopped | ½ |
| ¼ | yellow pepper, cored, seeded and chopped | ½ |
| ½ | small courgette, chopped | 1 |
| ½ | carrot, peeled and chopped | 1 |
| ¼ | red onion, peeled and chopped | ½ |
| ½ | clove of garlic, crushed | 1 |
| 1.25 ml/¼ tsp | saffron threads | 2.5 ml/½ tsp |
| 1.25 ml/¼ tsp | ground coriander | 2.5 ml/½ tsp |
| 1.25 ml/¼ tsp | ground cumin | 2.5 ml/½ tsp |
| 1.25 ml/¼ tsp | ground cinnamon | 2.5 ml/½ tsp |
| 30 ml/2 tbsp | dry white wine | 60 ml/4 tbsp |
| 30 ml/2 tbsp | passata | 60 ml/4 tbsp |
| 30 ml/2 tbsp | water | 60 ml/4 tbsp |
| | salt and pepper | |
| 75 g/3 oz | instant couscous | 175 g/6 oz |
| ¼ | finely grated zest and juice of lemon | ½ |

## One

1. Place half of the oil in a large bowl with the celery, peppers, courgette, carrot, red onion and garlic, mixing well. Cover tightly and microwave on HIGH for about 2 minutes until just softened, stirring once halfway through the cooking time.

2. Add the saffron, spices, wine, passata, water and salt and pepper to taste. Cover tightly and microwave on HIGH for 3-4 minutes, stirring twice, until the vegetables are tender and the sauce is pulpy.

3. Meanwhile, place the couscous in a bowl with the remaining oil and the lemon juice and zest and pour

over boiling water according to the packet instructions. Leave for 5 minutes to allow the grains to swell.

4. Fluff the couscous with a fork, add the vegetables with their sauce and gently fold together. Spoon on to a warmed serving plate and serve at once with harissa, if you like.

## Two

1. Place half of the oil in a large bowl with the celery, peppers, courgette, carrot, red onion and garlic, mixing well. Cover tightly and microwave on HIGH for about 3 minutes until just softened, stirring once halfway through the cooking time.

2. Add the saffron, spices, wine, passata, water and salt and pepper to taste. Cover tightly and microwave on HIGH for 4-4½ minutes, stirring twice, until the vegetables are tender and the sauce is pulpy.

3. Meanwhile, place the couscous in a bowl with the remaining oil and the lemon juice and zest and pour over boiling water according to the packet instructions. Leave to stand, covered, for 5 minutes to allow the grains to swell.

4. Fluff the couscous with a fork, add the vegetables with their sauce and gently fold together. Spoon on to two warmed serving plates and serve at once with harissa, if you like.

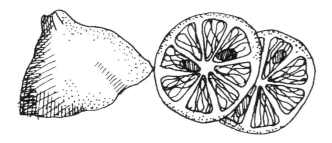

# End-of-the-Month Spaghettini

This is the recipe to make at the end of the month before the pay cheque arrives and when the refrigerator looks virtually bare. Needless to say, it doesn't taste a bit pauper-like - consider it cheap chic.

| One | | Two |
|---|---|---|
| 15 ml/1 tbsp | red wine vinegar | 30 ml/2 tbsp |
| 15 ml/1 tbsp | water | 30 ml/2 tbsp |
| scant 15 g/½ oz | sun-dried tomatoes (not in oil) | 20 g/¾ oz |
| 15 g/½ oz | black olives, stoned | 25 g/1 oz |
| 15 ml/1 tbsp | extra-virgin olive oil | 30 ml/2 tbsp |
| | pinch of crushed dried red chilli | |
| ½ | clove of garlic, crushed | 1 |
| 5-10 ml/1-2 tsp | chopped fresh basil | 10-15 ml/2-3 tsp |
| 50 g/2 oz | dried spaghettini or very fine noodles | 100 g/4 oz |
| 600 ml/1 pt | boiling water | 900 ml/1½ pts |
| | salt and pepper | |

## One and Two

1. Place the vinegar and the water in a bowl and microwave on HIGH for 15-30 seconds until hot. Add the sun-dried tomatoes, mixing well and leave to soak for a few hours.

2. Drain and dry the tomatoes and cut into fine julienne.

3. Place the tomatoes and olives in a small individual serving bowl, or divide between two individual serving bowls with the oil, chilli, garlic and basil.

4. Place the spaghettini in a medium bowl and pour over the boiling water. Microwave on HIGH for about 6 minutes, stirring once, or until the spaghettini is just tender. Drain thoroughly, reserving a little of the cooking liquid.

5. Add the pasta to the serving bowl, or divide between the two bowls, with salt and pepper to taste and 15-30 ml/1-2 tbsp of the cooking liquid to moisten. Toss gently to mix the spaghettini with the flavourings and serve at once.

# Oodles of Noodles with a Coconut Splash

Here is a wonderful one-pot idea for noodles and vegetables to be cooked in a coconut-milk-based sauce. The recipe illustrates the successful merging of Thai, Chinese and Italian cuisine to make a memorable meal.

| One | | Two |
|---|---|---|
| 100 g/4 oz | dried egg noodles | 225 g/8 oz |
| 600 ml/1 pt | boiling water | 1.2 litres/2 pts |
| 10 ml/2 tsp | vegetable oil | 20 ml/4 tsp |
| 2 | spring onions, chopped | 4 |
| ½ | red pepper, cored, seeded and sliced | 1 |
| 25 g/1 oz | finely shredded red cabbage | 50 g/2 oz |
| 40 g/1½ oz | button mushrooms, sliced | 75 g/3 oz |
| 25 g/1 oz | mangetout, trimmed and halved | 50 g/2 oz |
| 15 ml/1 tbsp | chopped fresh basil | 30 ml/2 tbsp |
| 10 ml/2 tsp | chopped fresh mint | 20 ml/4 tsp |
| | Sauce: | |
| 75 ml/3 fl oz | unsweetened coconut milk | 175 ml/6 fl oz |
| 15 ml/1 tbsp | dry sherry | 30 ml/2 tbsp |
| 7.5 ml/1½ tsp | oyster sauce | 15 ml/1 tbsp |
| 7.5 ml/1½ tsp | light soy sauce | 15 ml/1 tbsp |
| 2.5 ml/½ tsp | Chinese chilli sauce | 5 ml/1 tsp |
| | salt and pepper | |
| 7.5 ml/1½ tsp | cornflour | 15 ml/1 tbsp |

## One

1. Place the noodles in a medium bowl and pour over the boiling water. Microwave on HIGH for 6 minutes, stirring once. Leave to stand for minutes before draining thoroughly.

2. Meanwhile, place the oil in a medium bowl with the spring onions and pepper. Cover and microwave on HIGH for 1 minute, until softened.

3. Add the red cabbage, mushrooms, mangetout and herbs, blending well. Cover and microwave on HIGH for 1½-2½ minutes, stirring once, until the vegetables are tender crisp.

4. Meanwhile, mix the coconut milk with the sherry, oyster sauce, soy sauce, Chinese chilli sauce and salt and pepper to taste. Add to the vegetable mixture with the cooked noodles and toss gently to mix. Microwave on HIGH for 1-2 minutes until the mixture is hot.

5. Mix the cornflour with a little water and stir into the noodle mixture, mixing well. Microwave on HIGH for a further 1 minute, stirring once, until the sauce thickens slightly and coats the noodle and vegetable mixture. Serve at once.

## Two

1. Place the noodles in a medium bowl and pour over the boiling water. Microwave on HIGH for 6 minutes, stirring once. Leave to stand for 3 minutes before draining thoroughly.

2. Meanwhile, place the oil in a large bowl with the spring onions and pepper. Cover and microwave on HIGH for 1½ minutes, until softened.

3. Add the red cabbage, mushrooms, mangetout and herbs, blending well. Cover and microwave on HIGH for 2½-4 minutes, stirring once, until the vegetables are tender crisp.

4. Meanwhile, mix the coconut milk with the sherry, oyster sauce, soy sauce, Chinese chilli sauce and salt and pepper to taste. Add to the vegetable mixture with the cooked noodles and toss gently to mix. Microwave on HIGH for 1½-3 minutes until the mixture is hot.

5. Mix the cornflour with a little water and stir into the noodle mixture, mixing well. Microwave on HIGH for a further 1½ minutes, stirring once, until the sauce thickens slightly and coats the noodle and vegetable mixture. Serve at once.

*Oodles of Noodles with a Coconut Splash, top (page 60) and Thai Sesame Hot Noodles, bottom (page 109)*

# *Cheesy Oat Crumble*

Simply look to your vegetable basket for the filling of this crumble. Almost any selection of root vegetables, fresh beans, celery and onions can be used, simply mix and match according to what is available and what you like.

| One | | Two |
|---|---|---|
| 175 g/6 oz | raw mixed vegetables | 350 g/12 oz |
| 15 ml/1 tbsp | water | 30 ml/2 tbsp |
| | salt and pepper | |
| 3.75 ml/¾ tsp | chopped fresh mixed herbs | 7.5 ml/1½ tsp |
| 15 g/½ oz | peanuts, coarsely chopped if large | 25 g/1 oz |
| 15-30 ml/1-2 tbsp | baked beans in tomato sauce | 30-60 ml/2-4 tbsp |
| | Topping: | |
| 25 g/1 oz | medium oatmeal | 50 g/2 oz |
| 15 g/½ oz | bran | 25 g/1 oz |
| 15 g/½ oz | butter or margarine | 25 g/1 oz |
| 15 g/½ oz | vegetarian Cheddar cheese, crumbled | 25 g/1 oz |
| 5 ml/1 tsp | chopped fresh parsley | 10 ml/2 tsp |
| | sliced tomatoes and parsley sprigs, to garnish | |

## One

1. Prepare the vegetables according to type by slicing or chopping into bite-sized pieces. Place in a medium bowl with the water, a pinch of salt and the herbs. Cover and microwave on HIGH for 3-4 minutes until tender, stirring once halfway through the cooking time. Drain thoroughly and mix with the peanuts and beans.

2. To make the topping, mix the oatmeal with the bran in a bowl. Rub in the butter or margarine until the mixture resembles coarse breadcrumbs. Add the cheese, parsley and salt and pepper to taste, mixing well.

3. Place the vegetable mixture in a small casserole or heatproof dish and sprinkle with the crumble topping. Microwave, uncovered, on HIGH for 2½-3½ minutes or until the crumble is slightly firm to the touch.

4. Allow to stand for 2 minutes before serving garnished with tomato slices and parsley sprigs.

## Two

1. Prepare the vegetables according to type by slicing or chopping into bite-sized pieces. Place in a medium bowl with the water, a pinch of salt and the herbs. Cover and microwave on HIGH for 6-8 minutes until tender, stirring once halfway through the cooking time. Drain thoroughly and mix with the peanuts and beans.

2. To make the topping, mix the oatmeal with the bran in a bowl. Rub in the butter or margarine until the mixture resembles coarse breadcrumbs. Add the cheese, parsley and salt and pepper to taste, mixing well.

3. Place the vegetable mixture in a medium casserole or heatproof dish and sprinkle with the crumble topping. Microwave, uncovered, on HIGH for 5-7 minutes or until the crumble is slightly firm to the touch.

4. Allow to stand for 2 minutes before serving garnished with tomato slices and parsley sprigs.

*Blackeye Bean and Aubergine Curry (page 70) with Cucumber Raita and Poppadums (page 111)*

# Fast-Lane Curried Eggs

Here is a recipe for a quick curry that can be made faster than the time it takes to order the same from a local takeaway. Serve with rice, chutney and poppadoms (see page 111), for an authentic touch.

| One | | Two |
|---|---|---|
| ¼ | onion, peeled and chopped | ½ |
| ½ | clove of garlic, crushed | 1 |
| ½ | small aubergine, sliced and cut into bite-sized pieces | 1 |
| 1 | small courgettes, sliced | 2 |
| 1.25-2.5 ml/ ¼ - ½ tsp | curry powder | 2.5-5 ml/ ½ - 1 tsp |
| 1 | tomatoes, skinned, seeded and chopped | 2 |
| 37.5 ml/ 2½ tbsp | boiling vegetable stock or water | 75 ml/ 5 tbsp |
| 15 ml/1 tbsp | mango chutney | 30 ml/2 tbsp |
| 1 | hard-boiled eggs, shelled and cut into wedges or sliced | 2 |
| | salt and pepper | |

## One

1. Place the onion, garlic, aubergine, courgette and curry powder, to taste, in a medium bowl, mixing well. Cover and microwave on HIGH for 3-4 minutes, stirring once halfway through the cooking time, until the vegetables are tender.

2. Add the tomato and stock or water. Cover and microwave on HIGH for a further 1½-2 minutes.

3. Add the mango chutney and mix well to blend. Add the egg and salt and pepper to taste and microwave on HIGH for 1-1½ minutes to heat through, stirring once.

4. Serve hot with rice, chutney and poppadoms, if you like.

## Two

1. Place the onion, garlic, aubergine, courgette and curry powder, to taste, in a medium bowl, mixing well. Cover and microwave on HIGH for 6-8 minutes, stirring once halfway through the cooking time, until the vegetables are tender.

2. Add the tomatoes and stock or water. Cover and microwave on HIGH for a further 3-4 minutes.

3. Add the mango chutney and mix well to blend. Add the eggs and salt and pepper to taste and microwave on HIGH for 2½-3 minutes to heat through, stirring once.

4. Serve hot with rice, chutney and poppadoms, if you like.

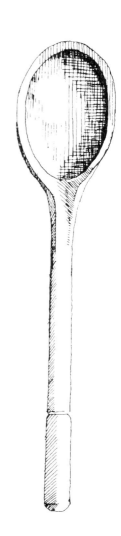

# *Root and Barley One-Pot*

This colourful barley and root vegetable one-pot dish makes a delicious and economical main meal. Ring the changes by replacing the basil with thyme, rosemary or a mixture of Provence-style fresh herbs. Toast the barley before cooking if you prefer.

| One | | Two |
|---|---|---|
| 40 g/1½ oz | pot barley | 75 g/3 oz |
| | boiling water to cover | |
| ½ | onion, peeled and chopped | 1 |
| 1 | small carrots, peeled and sliced | 2 |
| 40 g/1½ oz | swede, peeled and chopped | 75 g/3 oz |
| 1 | small courgettes, trimmed and sliced | 2 |
| ¼ | red pepper, cored, seeded and chopped | ½ |
| 150 ml/¼ pt | boiling vegetable stock | 300 ml/½ pt |
| 7.5 ml/1½ tsp | tomato paste | 15 ml/1 tbsp |
| 1 small | bay leaf | 1 |
| 5 ml/1 tsp | chopped fresh basil | 10 ml/2 tsp |
| | salt and pepper | |
| 25 g/1 oz | mushrooms, wiped and sliced | 50 g/2 oz |

## One

1. Place the barley in a medium bowl and add sufficient boiling water to cover. Leave to stand for 10 minutes.

2. Meanwhile, place the onion, carrot and swede in a medium dish, cover and microwave on HIGH for 2 minutes, stirring once. Add the courgette and red pepper, mixing well.

3. Drain the barley and add to the vegetables with the stock, tomato paste, bay leaf, basil and salt and pepper to taste, mixing well.

4. Cover and microwave on MEDIUM for 35-40 minutes, stirring twice, or until the barley is tender.

5. Stir in the mushrooms, re-cover and leave to stand for 5-10 minutes. Fluff with a fork to separate the barley grains and serve at once.

## Two

1. Place the barley in a medium bowl and add sufficient boiling water to cover. Leave to stand for 10 minutes.

2 . Meanwhile, place the onion, carrot and swede in a medium dish, cover and microwave on HIGH for 4 minutes, stirring once. Add the courgette and red pepper, mixing well.

3. Drain the barley and add to the vegetables with the stock, tomato paste, bay leaf, basil and salt and pepper to taste, mixing well.

4. Cover and microwave on MEDIUM for 35-40 minutes, stirring twice, or until the barley is tender.

5. Stir in the mushrooms, re-cover and leave to stand for 5-10 minutes. Fluff with a fork to separate the barley grains and serve at once.

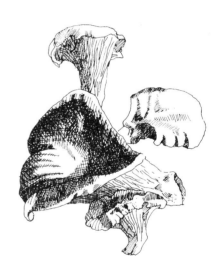

# Aubergine and Butter-Bean Crumble

This really is a one-pot dish of savoury vegetables and beans with a crunchy crumble topping. Serve with a crisp seasonal salad for a light but nourishing main meal.

| One | | Two |
|---|---|---|
| ¼ | onion, peeled and chopped | ½ |
| | knob of butter or margarine | |
| ½ | beef tomato, chopped | 1 |
| ½ | small aubergine, weighing about 225 g/8 oz, thinly sliced | 1 |
| ½ | 200 g/7 oz can butter beans, drained and rinsed | 1 |
| | salt and pepper | |
| 45 ml/3 tbsp | fresh white or wholemeal breadcrumbs | 90 ml/6 tbsp |
| 7.5 ml/1½ tsp | chopped fresh parsley | 15 ml/1 tbsp |
| 7.5 ml/1½ tsp | sunflower seeds | 15 ml/1 tbsp |
| 10 ml/2 tsp | unsalted peanuts, chopped | 20 ml/4 tsp |

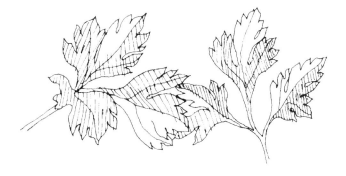

## One

1. Place the onion and butter or margarine in a dish, cover and microwave on HIGH for 45-60 seconds, stirring once.

2. Add the tomato and aubergine, re-cover and microwave on HIGH for 2-2½ minutes, or until the aubergine is just tender, stirring once.

3. Stir in the beans and season with salt and pepper to taste. Spoon into a small heatproof serving dish.

4. To make the topping, mix the breadcrumbs with the parsley, sunflower seeds, peanuts and salt and pepper to taste, mixing well. Spoon over the aubergine and bean mixture to coat evenly. Microwave on HIGH for 1-2 minutes or until heated through. Brown and crisp under a preheated hot grill if you like. Serve hot.

## Two

1. Place the onion and butter or margarine in a dish, cover and microwave on HIGH for 1-1½ minutes, stirring once.

2. Add the tomato and aubergine, re-cover and microwave on HIGH for 3-3½ minutes, or until the aubergine is tender, stirring once.

3. Stir in the beans and season with salt and pepper to taste. Spoon into a medium heatproof serving dish.

4. To make the topping, mix the breadcrumbs with the parsley, sunflower seeds, peanuts and salt and pepper to taste, mixing well. Spoon over the aubergine and bean mixture to coat evenly. Microwave on HIGH for 2-3 minutes or until heated through. Brown and crisp under a preheated hot grill if you like. Serve hot.

# Smoked Tofu Kedgeree

This is a wonderfully colourful and aromatic dish of long-grain brown rice flavoured with garam masala and studded with cooked peas, sweetcorn, red peppers and cubes of smoked tofu. Save it for a special occasion.

| One | | Two |
|---|---|---|
| 50 ml/2 fl oz | vegetable stock | 100 ml/4 fl oz |
| 1 | large red peppers, cored, seeded and sliced | 2 |
| 50 ml/2 fl oz | creamy milk | 100 ml/4 fl oz |
| 7.5 ml/1½ tsp | garam masala | 15 ml/1 tbsp |
| 40 g/1½ oz | frozen peas | 75 g/3 oz |
| 40 g/1½ oz | frozen sweetcorn | 75 g/3 oz |
| 100 g/4 oz | cooked long-grain brown rice | 225 g/8 oz |
| 25 g/1 oz | mushrooms, wiped and sliced | 50 g/2 oz |
| 100 g/4 oz | smoked tofu, cubed | 225 g/8 oz |
| | salt and pepper | |
| | chopped parsley, to garnish | |

## One

1. Place the stock and the pepper in a large bowl. Cover and microwave on HIGH for 2 minutes, until softened.

2. Add the milk and garam masala, mixing well. Cover and microwave on HIGH for a further 1 minute.

3. Add the peas and sweetcorn, mixing well. Cover and microwave on HIGH for 2-3 minutes, or until just cooked, stirring once.

4. Add the rice and mix well to combine. Stir in the mushrooms, tofu and salt and pepper to taste, taking care not to break up the tofu. Cover and microwave on HIGH for a further 1-2 minutes, until very hot, stirring once.

5. Serve hot, sprinkled with chopped parsley.

## Two

1. Place the stock and the peppers in a large bowl. Cover and microwave on HIGH for 3 minutes, until softened.

2. Add the milk and garam masala, mixing well. Cover and microwave on HIGH for a further 1-1½ minutes.

3. Add the peas and sweetcorn, mixing well. Cover and microwave on HIGH for 3-4 minutes, or until just cooked, stirring once.

4. Add the rice and mix well to combine. Stir in the mushrooms, tofu and salt and pepper to taste, taking care not to break up the tofu. Cover and microwave on HIGH for a further 1½-2 minutes, until very hot, stirring once.

5. Serve hot, sprinkled with chopped parsley.

# Warm Broad Bean, Lemon Olive and Mozzarella Salad

This is a tasty main course salad that has more than a hint of tropical climes. Serve with sun-dried tomato or olive bread for a truly Mediterranean feast.

## One                                                          Two

| One | | Two |
|---|---|---|
| 75 g/3 oz | fresh shelled broad beans | 175 g/6 oz |
| 30 ml/2 tbsp | water | 60 ml/4 tbsp |
| 5 ml/1 tsp | olive oil | 10 ml/2 tsp |
| ½ | small clove of garlic, crushed | 1 |
| 3.75 ml/¾ tsp | balsamic vinegar | 7.5 ml/1½ tsp |
| 40 g/1½ oz | vegetarian Mozzarella cheese, sliced | 75 g/3 oz |
| 15 g/½ oz | sun-dried tomatoes in oil, coarsely chopped | 25 g/1 oz |
| 15 g/½ oz | lemon olives | 25 g/1 oz |
| 7.5 ml/1½ tsp | chopped fresh mixed herbs (basil, thyme, rosemary, chervil and parsley, for example) | 15 ml/1 tbsp |
| | salt and pepper | |

## One

1. Place the broad beans in a dish with the water. Cover and microwave on HIGH for 3-3½ minutes, stirring once, until tender. Leave to stand while preparing the garlic oil.

2. Place the oil and the garlic in a bowl and microwave on HIGH for 30 seconds. Drain the beans and add to the garlic oil with the vinegar. Cover and microwave on HIGH for a further 30 seconds.

3. Add the cheese, tomatoes, olives, herbs and salt and pepper to taste, mixing well. Serve at once with crusty sun-dried tomato or olive bread.

## Two

1. Place the broad beans in a dish with the water. Cover and microwave on HIGH for 4½-5½ minutes, stirring once, until tender. Leave to stand while preparing the garlic oil.

2. Place the oil and the garlic in a bowl and microwave on HIGH for 30 seconds. Drain the beans and add to the garlic oil with the vinegar. Cover and microwave on HIGH for a further 45-60 seconds.

3. Add the cheese, tomatoes, olives, herbs and salt and pepper to taste, mixing well. Serve at once with crusty sun-dried tomato or olive bread.

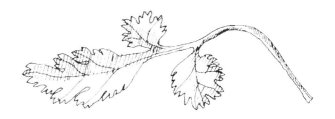

# Ratatouille in a Rush

This is the speediest way I know to make a flavoursome ratatouille that is just perfect for serving, dusting with grated Parmesan, with a huge chunk of crusty bread. It is such a versatile dish that you can use it to fill omelettes, lasagnes, baked pie crusts (made from either pastry or rice) and to top cooked rice and pasta.

## One                                                          Two

| One | | Two |
|---|---|---|
| 7.5 ml/1½ tsp | olive oil | 15 ml/1 tbsp |
| ½ | onion, peeled and copped | 1 |
| 1 | cloves of garlic, crushed | 2 |
| 100 g/4 oz | aubergine, diced | 225 g/8 oz |
| ½ | yellow pepper, cored, seeded and sliced | 1 |
| 100 g/4 oz | courgettes, sliced | 225 g/8 oz |
| ½ | 400 g/14 oz carton passata | 1 |
| 7.5 ml/1½ tsp | tomato purée | 15 ml/1 tbsp |
| | small bay leaf | |
| 7.5 ml/1½ tsp | chopped mixed fresh herbs (parsley, basil, thyme and rosemary, for example) | 15 ml/1 tbsp |
| | salt and pepper | |
| | freshly grated Parmesan cheese, to serve (optional) | |

## One

1. Place the oil in a medium bowl with the onion and garlic. Microwave on HIGH for 2 minutes, stirring once.

2. Add the aubergine, pepper and courgettes, mixing well. Cover and microwave on HIGH for 2½ minutes, stirring once.

3. Add the passata, tomato purée, bay leaf, herbs and salt and pepper to taste. Stir well to mix, cover and microwave on HIGH for 4-5 minutes, stirring once.

4. Remove and discard the bay leaf and adjust the seasoning if necessary. Spoon into a serving bowl and dust the top with Parmesan cheese to serve, if you like.

## Two

1. Place the oil in a medium bowl with the onion and garlic. Microwave on HIGH for 3 minutes, stirring once.

2. Add the aubergine, pepper and courgettes, mixing well. Cover and microwave on HIGH for 4 minutes, stirring once.

3. Add the passata, tomato purée, bay leaf, herbs and salt and pepper to taste. Stir well to mix, cover and microwave on HIGH for 5-7 minutes, stirring once.

4. Remove and discard the bay leaf and adjust the seasoning if necessary. Spoon into a serving bowl and dust the top with Parmesan cheese to serve, if you like.

# Cheese and Wine Fondue

A fondue must be the epitome of a one-pot meal. All you need to complete this dish is some crusty bread dippers and perhaps a crisp seasonal salad.

| One | | Two |
| --- | --- | --- |
| 100 g/4 oz | Emmenthal cheese, grated | 225 g/8 oz |
| 100 g/4 oz | Gruyère cheese, grated | 225 g/8 oz |
| 22.5 ml/1½ tbsp | plain flour | 45 ml/3 tbsp |
| ½ | clove of garlic, peeled and crushed | 1 |
| | pinch of grated nutmeg | |
| 125 ml/4 fl oz | dry white wine | 250 ml/8 fl oz |
| | pepper | |
| | crusty bread cubes, to serve | |

## One

1. Shake the cheeses, flour, garlic and nutmeg together in a plastic bag.

2. Place the wine in a medium serving bowl and stir in the cheese mixture. Microwave on MEDIUM for 4-5 minutes, or until hot and bubbly stirring about 3 times to keep the mixture smooth and thickened.

3. Add pepper to taste and serve at once with the crusty bread cubes as dippers.

## Two

1. Shake the cheeses, flour, garlic and nutmeg together in a plastic bag.

2. Place the wine in a medium serving bowl and stir in the cheese mixture. Microwave on MEDIUM for 6-8 minutes, or until hot and bubbly stirring about 3 times to keep the mixture smooth and thickened.

3. Add pepper to taste and serve at once with the crusty bread cubes as dippers.

## Italian Wild-Mushroom Risotto

You don't have to use wild mushrooms for this recipe but the flavour and interest they create is worth the effort. If saffron is hard to find then use a pinch of ground turmeric instead.

| One | | Two |
| --- | --- | --- |
| 5 ml/1 tsp | olive oil | 10 ml/2 tsp |
| ¼ | small onion, peeled and chopped | ½ |
| ¼ | small bulb of fennel, very finely sliced | ½ |
| 60 g/2½ oz | Italian arborio or risotto rice | 150 g/5 oz |
| 150 ml/¼ pt | hot vegetable stock | 300 ml/½ pt |
| | small pinch of saffron threads | |
| 75 ml/5 tbsp | dry white wine | 150 ml/¼ pt |
| 75 g/3 oz | wild mushrooms, sliced | 175 g/6 oz |
| 50 g/2 oz | baby asparagus tips | 100 g/4 oz |
| 15 g/½ oz | vegetarian Parmesan cheese, grated | 25 g/1 oz |
| | salt and pepper | |

## One

1. Place the oil, onion and fennel in a medium bowl, mixing well. Cover and microwave on HIGH for 1 minute until softened. Stir in the rice, mixing well.

2. Mix the stock with the saffron and wine. Add 75 ml/5 tbsp of the mixture to the rice and stir well. Microwave, uncovered, on HIGH for about 2 minutes or until the liquid is absorbed. Add a further 50 ml/2 fl oz of the liquid and mix well. Microwave on HIGH for a further 2 minutes. Repeat using a further 50 ml/2 fl oz of the liquid.

3. Stir the remaining liquid into the rice mixture with the mushrooms and asparagus, mixing well. Microwave, uncovered, on HIGH for a further 3 minutes or until the rice grains, mushrooms and asparagus are tender, stirring every 1 minute. (If the mixture becomes a little dry, then add a little extra stock or wine.)

4. Stir in the Parmesan cheese and salt and pepper to taste and microwave on HIGH for a further ½ - 1 minute or until the cheese has melted. Serve at once.

## Two

1. Place the oil, onion and fennel in a large bowl,

mixing well. Cover and microwave on HIGH for 1½ minutes until softened. Stir in the rice, mixing well.

2. Mix the stock with the saffron and wine. Add 150 ml/¼ pt of the mixture to the rice and stir well. Microwave, uncovered, on HIGH for 3 minutes or until the liquid is absorbed. Add a further 100 ml/3 ½ fl oz of the liquid and mix well. Microwave on HIGH for a further 3 minutes. Repeat using a further 100 ml/3 ½ fl oz of the liquid.

3. Stir the remaining liquid into the rice mixture with the mushrooms and asparagus, mixing well. Microwave, uncovered, on HIGH for a further 5 minutes or until the rice grains, mushrooms and asparagus are tender, stirring 3 times during the cooking. (If the mixture becomes a little dry, then add a little extra stock or wine.)

4. Stir in the Parmesan cheese and salt and pepper to taste and microwave on HIGH for a further 1-1½ minutes or until the cheese has melted. Serve at once.

# Saffron Risotto with Leeks, Mangetout and Asparagus

I adore the flavour of saffron and, although expensive to buy, it does lift even the simplest dish from the everyday to the luxury class. In this dish, saffron-flavoured rice is cooked with baby asparagus, mange tout and leeks to make an unforgettable risotto.

| One | | Two |
|---|---|---|
| 5 ml/1 tsp | olive oil | 10 ml/2 tsp |
| ¼ | onion, peeled and chopped | ½ |
| 1 | baby leeks, washed and sliced | 2 |
| 60 g/2½ oz | Italian arborio or risotto rice | 150 g/5 oz |
| 150 ml/¼ pt | hot vegetable stock | 300 ml/½ pt |
| | small pinch of saffron threads | |
| 75 ml/5 tbsp | dry white wine | 150 ml/¼ pt |
| 50 g/2 oz | mangetout, sliced diagonally | 100 g/4 oz |
| 50 g/2 oz | baby asparagus tips, trimmed | 100 g/4 oz |
| | salt and pepper | |

## One

1. Place the oil, onion and leek in a medium bowl, mixing well. Cover and microwave on HIGH for 1 minute until softened. Stir in the rice, mixing well.

2. Mix the stock with the saffron and wine. Add 75 ml/5 tbsp of the mixture to the rice and stir well. Microwave, uncovered, on HIGH for about 2 minutes or until the liquid is absorbed. Add a further 50 ml/2 fl oz of the liquid and mix well. Microwave on HIGH for a further 2 minutes. Repeat using a further 50 ml/2 fl oz of the liquid.

3. Stir the remaining liquid into the rice mixture with the mange tout and asparagus tips, mixing well. Microwave, uncovered, on HIGH for a further 3 minutes or until the rice grains, mangetout and asparagus are tender, stirring every 1 minute. (If the mixture becomes a little dry then add a little extra stock or wine.)

4. Add salt and pepper to taste, mixing well. Serve at once.

## Two

1. Place the oil, onion and leeks in a medium bowl, mixing well. Cover and microwave on HIGH for 1½ minutes until softened. Stir in the rice, mixing well.

2. Mix the stock with the saffron and wine. Add 150 ml/¼ pt of the mixture to the rice and stir well. Microwave, uncovered, on HIGH for 3 minutes or until the liquid is absorbed. Add a further 100 ml/3½ fl oz of the liquid and mix well. Microwave on HIGH for a further 3 minutes. Repeat using a further 100 ml/3½ fl oz of the liquid.

3. Stir the remaining liquid into the rice mixture with the mange tout and asparagus tips, mixing well. Microwave, uncovered, on HIGH for a further 5 minutes or until the rice grains, mangetout and asparagus are tender, stirring 3 times during cooking. (If the mixture becomes a little dry then add a little extra stock or wine.)

4. Add salt and pepper to taste, mixing well. Serve at once.

# Aubergine and Tomato with Fennel

This is a super main-course meal that is perfect for serving with a mixed green salad and some crusty bread. Cooked in the microwave the vegetables in this dish stay plump and the juices they produce are rich and flavourful.

| One | | Two |
| --- | --- | --- |
| 2 | small aubergines | 4 |
| 2 | large plum tomatoes | 4 |
| ¼ | bulb of fennel | ½ |
| 2 | large cloves of garlic, crushed | 4 |
| 1 | sprigs of fresh basil | 2 |
| | pinch of fresh or dried thyme | |
| 15 ml/1 tbsp | extra virgin olive oil | 30 ml/2 tbsp |
| 7.5 ml/1½ tsp | water | 15 ml/1 tbsp |
| | salt and pepper | |

## One

1. Thickly slice the aubergines and tomatoes and layer in a shallow medium dish. Scatter the fennel on top and tuck the garlic, basil leaves and thyme between all of the vegetables.

2. Mix the oil with the water and salt and pepper to taste and drizzle over the top of the vegetables. Cover tightly and microwave on HIGH for 10 minutes.

3. Leave to stand, covered, for 3 minutes, before serving with a crisp green salad and bread for mopping up the juices.

## Two

1. Thickly slice the aubergines and tomatoes and layer in a medium to large shallow dish. Scatter the fennel on top and tuck the garlic, basil leaves and thyme between all of the vegetables.

2. Mix the oil with the water and salt and pepper

to taste and drizzle over the top of the vegetables. Cover tightly and microwave on HIGH for 15 minutes.

3. Leave to stand, covered, for 3 minutes, before serving with a crisp green salad and bread for mopping up the juices.

# Blackeye Bean and Aubergine Curry

This is a full-bodied hot curry dish perfect for serving with rice and typical curry accompaniments like poppadoms, cucumber raita and mango chutney.

| One | | Two |
| --- | --- | --- |
| 50 g/2 oz | dried blackeye beans, soaked overnight in cold water | 100 g/4 oz |
| | boiling water to cover | |
| 225 g/8 oz | aubergines, cut into 2.5-cm/1-inch cubes | 450 g/1 lb |
| ½ | juice of lemon | 1 |
| 30 ml/2 tbsp | vegetable oil | 60 ml/4 tbsp |
| ½ | onion, peeled and thinly sliced | 1 |
| ½ | clove of garlic, crushed | 1 |
| 1 | green chillies, seeded and finely chopped | 2 |
| 2.5 ml/½ tsp | coriander seeds | 5 ml/1 tsp |
| 15 ml/1 tbsp | garam masala | 30 ml/2 tbsp |
| 2.5 ml/½ tsp | turmeric | 5 ml/1 tsp |
| | salt and pepper | |
| 50 g/2 oz | canned tomatoes, chopped | 100 g/4 oz |
| | fresh coriander, to garnish | |

## One

1. Rinse and drain the blackeye beans and place in a medium bowl and add sufficient boiling water to cover. Cover and microwave on HIGH for 10 minutes.

2. Meanwhile, place the aubergine cubes in a bowl, add the lemon juice and mix well.

3. Reduce the power setting to MEDIUM and cook the beans for a further 5 minutes.

4. Add the aubergines and lemon juice to the beans, mixing well. Cover and microwave on MEDIUM for a further 6-10 minutes or until the beans are just tender, adding a little more boiling water if necessary. Drain thoroughly.

5. Place the oil in a large bowl with the onion, garlic and chilli. Cover tightly and microwave on HIGH for 1 minute until just softened. Add the spices with a good grinding of black pepper, mixing well. Cover and microwave on HIGH for 1-2 minutes to cook the spices.

6. Add the bean and aubergine mixture with the tomatoes, mixing well. Cover and microwave on HIGH for 3-4 minutes until the curry is thick and pulpy. Add salt to taste and serve with rice and curry accompaniments.

## Two

1. Rinse and drain the blackeye beans and place in a medium bowl and add sufficient boiling water to cover. Cover and microwave on HIGH for 10 minutes.

2. Meanwhile, place the aubergine cubes in a bowl, add the lemon juice and mix well.

3. Reduce the power setting to MEDIUM and cook the beans for a further 5 minutes.

4. Add the aubergines and lemon juice to the beans, mixing well. Cover and microwave on MEDIUM for a further 6-10 minutes or until the beans are just tender, adding a little more boiling water if necessary. Drain thoroughly.

5. Place the oil in a large bowl with the onion, garlic and chillies. Cover tightly and microwave on HIGH for 1½ minutes until just softened. Add the spices with a good grinding of black pepper, mixing well. Cover and microwave on HIGH for 1½-2½ minutes to cook the spices.

6. Add the bean and aubergine mixture with the tomatoes, mixing well. Cover and microwave on HIGH for 4-5 minutes, until the curry is thick and pulpy. Add salt to taste and serve with rice and curry accompaniments.

# Luxury Macaroni Cheese

This is the tastiest macaroni cheese around, for it is made with not one but three cheeses. Vegetarian cheddar, mozzarella and Parmesan. Flash under a preheated hot grill to brown and crisp the topping just before serving. Serve with a crisp seasonal salad.

| One | | Two |
|---|---|---|
| 50 g/2 oz | macaroni | 100 g/4 oz |
| 450 ml/¾ pt | boiling water | 600 ml/1 pt |
| 15 g/½ oz | butter | 25 g/1 oz |
| 11.25 ml/2¼ tsp | plain flour | 22.5 ml/4½ tsp |
| | pinch of ground bay leaves | |
| 125 ml/4 fl oz | milk | 250 ml/8 fl oz |
| 50 g/2 oz | vegetarian Cheddar cheese, grated | 100 g/4 oz |
| 2.5 ml/½ tsp | Dijon mustard | 5 ml/1 tsp |
| | salt and pepper | |
| 25 g/1 oz | mozzarella cheese, coarsely chopped | 50 g/2 oz |
| 15 g/½ oz | vegetarian Parmesan cheese, grated | 25 g/1 oz |
| 15 ml/1 tbsp | fresh white breadcrumbs | 30 ml/2 tbsp |

## One

1. Place the macaroni in a medium bowl and pour over the boiling water. Microwave on HIGH for 10 minutes, stirring once halfway through the cooking time until the pasta is just tender. Leave to stand for 3 minutes before draining thoroughly.

2. Place the butter in a large measuring jug with the flour, ground bay leaf and milk, mixing well. Microwave on HIGH for 2½-3 minutes, beating every 1 minute, until smooth, boiling and thickened.

3. Add the Cheddar cheese, mustard and salt and pepper to taste, blending well.

4. Add to the cooked macaroni with the mozzarella cheese and half of the Parmesan. Microwave on HIGH for a further 1 minute until hot and bubbly.

5. Spoon into a small flameproof dish, then sprinkle with the breadcrumbs and remaining Parmesan.

6. Cook under a preheated hot grill until golden and bubbly. Alternatively microwave on HIGH for a further 1 minute until hot and bubbly. Serve hot with a crisp seasonal salad.

## Two

1. Place the macaroni in a large bowl and pour over the boiling water. Microwave on HIGH for 10 minutes, stirring once halfway through the cooking time until the pasta is just tender. Leave to stand for 3 minutes before draining thoroughly.

2. Place the butter in a large measuring jug with the flour, ground bay leaf and milk, mixing well. Microwave on HIGH for 3½ - 4 minutes, beating every 1 minute, until smooth, boiling and thickened.

3. Add the Cheddar cheese, mustard and salt and pepper to taste, blending well.

4. Add to the cooked macaroni with the mozzarella cheese and half of the Parmesan. Microwave on HIGH for a further 1½ minutes until hot and bubbly.

5. Spoon into a medium flameproof dish, then sprinkle with the breadcrumbs and remaining Parmesan.

6. Cook under a preheated hot grill until golden and bubbly. Alternatively microwave on HIGH for a further 1 - 1½ minutes until hot and bubbly. Serve hot with a crisp seasonal salad.

# Thai Noodles with Vegetables and Tofu

It is essential to use rice noodles for this recipe. They can be found in many supermarkets and specialist shops and are often called rice sticks or rice vermicelli. They do not need boiling for use but are simply soaked in hot water before adding to savoury vegetable mixtures and stir-fries.

| One | | Two |
|---|---|---|
| 40 g/1½ oz | dried Thai rice noodles | 75 g/3 oz |
| 7.5 ml/1½ tsp | sunflower oil | 15 ml/1 tbsp |
| ½ | clove of garlic, crushed | 1 |
| ¼ | small red pepper, cored, seeded and sliced | ½ |
| ¼ | small yellow pepper, cored seeded and sliced | ½ |
| ½ | small courgette, cut into matchsticks | 1 |
| 1 | small tomatoes, coarsely chopped | 2 |
| 50 g/2 oz | firm tofu, cubed | 100 g/4 oz |
| 25 g/1 oz | beansprouts | 50 g/2 oz |
| 1 | spring onions, finely chopped | 2 |
| | pinch of cayenne pepper | |
| 7.5 ml/1½ tsp | soy sauce | 15 ml/1 tbsp |
| | lime juice, to taste | |
| | salt and pepper | |

## One

1. Soak the rice noodles in warm water until softened, about 10 minutes (or according to the packet instructions). Drain thoroughly.

2. Place the oil and garlic in a large bowl and microwave on HIGH for 30 seconds.

3. Add the peppers and microwave on HIGH for 30 seconds.

4. Add the courgette and microwave on HIGH for a further 15 seconds.

5. Add the tomato, tofu, rice noodles, beansprouts, spring onions, cayenne and soy sauce, mixing well. Microwave on HIGH for 1-2 minutes, stirring twice, until the vegetables are cooked tender crisp.

6. Add lime juice and salt and pepper to taste, mixing well. Transfer to a warmed serving dish and serve at once.

## Two

1. Soak the rice noodles in warm water until softened, about 10 minutes (or according to the packet instructions). Drain thoroughly.

2. Place the oil and garlic in a large bowl and microwave on HIGH for 30-45 seconds.

3. Add the peppers and microwave on HIGH for 30-45 seconds.

4. Add the courgette and microwave on HIGH for a further 15-30 seconds.

5. Add the tomatoes, tofu, rice noodles, beansprouts, spring onions, cayenne and soy sauce, mixing well. Microwave on HIGH for 1½-2½ minutes, stirring twice, until the vegetables are cooked tender crisp.

6. Add lime juice and salt and pepper to taste, mixing well. Divide between two individual warmed serving dishes and serve at once.

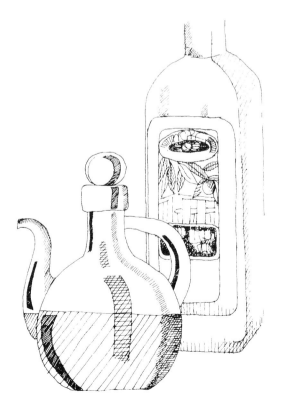

# *Chinese Quorn Stir Fry*

The microwave can't stir fry in the traditional sense but it will cook vegetables tender crisp and in the stir-fry fashion. If you prefer cook this recipe in a preheated browning dish to introduce a more golden colour to the Quorn and vegetables.

| One | | Two |
|---|---|---|
| 7.5 ml/1½ tsp | vegetable oil | 15 ml/1 tbsp |
| 75 g/3 oz | Quorn pieces | 175 g/6 oz |
| ½ | clove of garlic, peeled and chopped | 1 |
| ½ | red pepper, cored, seeded and chopped | 1 |
| 2 | spring onions, trimmed and chopped | 4 |
| 7.5 ml/1½ tsp | dry sherry | 15 ml/1 tbsp |
| 50 g/2 oz | beansprouts | 100 g/4 oz |
| 25 g/1 oz | blanched tiny broccoli florets | 50 g/2 oz |
| 25 g/1 oz | dwarf baby sweetcorn, halved | 50 g/2 oz |
| 3.75 ml/¾ tsp | cornflour | 7.5 ml/1½ tsp |
| 50 ml/2 fl oz | vegetable stock | 125 ml/4 fl oz |
| 15 ml/1 tbsp | dark soy sauce | 30 ml/2 tbsp |
| 7.5 ml/1½ tsp | Hoisin sauce | 15 ml/1 tbsp |

## One

1. Place the oil in a large shallow dish and microwave on HIGH for 15-30 seconds until very hot. Add the Quorn pieces and microwave on HIGH for 30-60 seconds, stirring twice. Alternatively, preheat a browning dish according to the manufacturer's instructions, add the oil and swirl to coat, then add the Quorn pieces and turn on all sides to brown evenly.

2. Add the garlic, red pepper and spring onions, cover and microwave on HIGH for 1 minute.

3. Add the sherry, beansprouts, broccoli and sweetcorn, cover and microwave on HIGH for 1-1½ minutes or until the vegetables are tender crisp.

4. Mix the cornflour with the stock, soy sauce and Hoisin sauce, blending well. Stir into the vegetable mixture. Re-cover and microwave on HIGH for a further 1-2 minutes, stirring every 30 seconds until

the sauce is thickened and glossy and coats the tender crisp vegetables and Quorn. Serve at once with a rice or noodle accompaniment if you like.

## Two

1. Place the oil in a large shallow dish and microwave on HIGH for 15-30 seconds until very hot. Add the Quorn pieces and microwave on HIGH for about 1 minute, stirring twice. Alternatively, preheat a large browning dish according to the manufacturer's instructions, add the oil and swirl to coat, then add the Quorn pieces and turn on all sides to brown evenly.

2. Add the garlic, red pepper and spring onions, cover and microwave on HIGH for 1½ minutes.

3. Add the sherry, beansprouts, broccoli and sweetcorn, cover and microwave on HIGH for 1½-2½ minutes or until the vegetables are tender crisp.

4. Mix the cornflour with the stock, soy sauce and Hoisin sauce, blending well. Stir into the vegetable mixture. Re-cover and microwave on HIGH for a further 1½-2½ minutes, stirring every 30 seconds until the sauce is thickened and glossy and coats the tender crisp vegetables and Quorn. Serve at once with a rice or noodle accompaniment if you like.

## Mr McGregor's Lasagne

I don't think for one minute that Mr McGregor would have grown red peppers and courgettes in his vegetable garden but since we're talking fiction here, then let's pretend he did.

| One | | Two |
|---|---|---|
| ½ | onion, peeled and chopped | 1 |
| ½ | clove of garlic, crushed | 1 |
| ¼ | red pepper, cored, seeded and chopped | ½ |
| 100 g/4 oz | tomatoes, skinned and chopped | 225 g/8 oz |
| 50 g/2 oz | courgettes, trimmed and sliced | 100 g/4 oz |
| 1.25 ml/¼ tsp | chopped fresh basil | 2.5 ml/½ tsp |
| | salt and pepper | |
| 50 g/2 oz | mushrooms, wiped and sliced | 100 g/4 oz |
| knob | butter or margarine | 20 g/¾ oz |
| 11.25 ml/2 ¼ tsp | flour | 22.5 ml/1½ tbsp |
| 75 ml/5 tbsp | milk | 150 ml/¼ pt |
| 37.5 ml/2½ tbsp | natural yogurt | 75 ml/5 tbsp |
| 25 g/1 oz | vegetarian Cheddar cheese, grated | 50 g/2 oz |
| 15 g/½ oz | vegetarian Parmesan cheese, grated | 25 g/1 oz |
| 50 g/2 oz | dried lasagne | 100 g/4 oz |
| 5 ml/1 tsp | oil | 5 ml/1 tsp |
| | boiling water to cover | |
| 15 ml/1 tbsp | sunflower seeds | 30 ml/2 tbsp |

## One

1. Place the onion and garlic in a medium bowl, cover and microwave on HIGH for 1 minute, stirring once. Add the red pepper, re-cover and microwave on HIGH for a further 45 seconds.

2. Add the tomatoes, courgettes, basil and salt and pepper to taste, mixing well. Cover and microwave on HIGH for 3-3½ minutes, stirring once. Add the mushrooms and microwave on HIGH, uncovered, for 2 minutes, stirring once. Keep warm while preparing the sauce.

3. Place the butter or margarine in a jug with the flour and milk, mixing well. Microwave on HIGH for 1¼ - 2 minutes, stirring every 30 seconds, or until the sauce is smooth, boiling and thickened. Add the yogurt, Cheddar cheese and half of the Parmesan, mixing well.

4. Place the lasagne in a large dish with the oil and sufficient boiling water to cover. Cover and microwave on HIGH for 2 minutes, then leave to stand for 2 minutes. Drain thoroughly.

5. Layer the vegetable mixture in a heatproof dish with the lasagne, starting with a vegetable layer and finishing with a pasta layer. Spoon over the cheesy sauce to coat and sprinkle with the remaining Parmesan cheese and sunflower seeds. Microwave on MEDIUM for 6-8 minutes or until the pasta is cooked and the lasagne is hot and bubbly. Brown under a preheated hot grill until golden if you wish before serving.

## Two

1. Place the onion and garlic in a medium bowl, cover and microwave on HIGH for 1½ minutes, stirring once. Add the red pepper, re-cover and microwave on HIGH for a further 1 minute.

2. Add the tomatoes, courgettes, basil and salt and pepper to taste, mixing well. Cover and microwave on HIGH for 6-7 minutes, stirring once. Add the mushrooms and microwave on HIGH, uncovered, for 3 minutes, stirring once. Keep warm while preparing the sauce.

3. Place the butter or margarine in a jug with the flour and milk, mixing well. Microwave on HIGH for 2½ - 3½ minutes, stirring every 30 seconds, or until the sauce is smooth, boiling and thickened. Add the yogurt, Cheddar cheese and half of the Parmesan, mixing well.

4. Place the lasagne in a large dish with the oil and sufficient boiling water to cover. Cover and microwave on HIGH for 2 minutes, then leave to stand for 2 minutes. Drain thoroughly.

5. Layer the vegetable mixture in a heatproof dish with the lasagne, starting with a vegetable layer and finishing with a pasta layer. Spoon over the cheesy

sauce to coat and sprinkle with the remaining Parmesan and sunflower seeds. Microwave on MEDIUM for 6-8 minutes or until the pasta is cooked and the lasagne is hot and bubbly. Brown under a preheated hot grill until golden if you wish before serving.

## Spicy Nut Cutlets

For success this recipe is best prepared in a browning dish so that the cutlets have a good colour and crisp texture when cooked.

| One | | Two |
|---|---|---|
| 40 g/1½ oz | cashew nuts, finely chopped | 75 g/3 oz |
| 15 g/½ oz | walnuts, finely chopped | 25 g/1 oz |
| 1 | shallots or small onions, peeled and finely chopped | 2 |
| 15 g/½ oz | fresh white or brown breadcrumbs | 25 g/1 oz |
| | pinch of ground turmeric | |
| | pinch of ground allspice | |
| 1.25 ml/¼ tsp | ground cumin | 2.5 ml/½ tsp |
| 5 ml/1 tsp | chopped fresh parsley | 10 ml/2 tsp |
| ½ | small egg, beaten | 1 |
| | salt and pepper | |
| | oil to brush | |

## One

1. Mix the cashews with the walnuts, shallot, breadcrumbs, spices, parsley, egg and salt and pepper to taste, mixing well. Divide and shape the mixture into 2 rounds or cutlet shapes, cover and chill for at least 1 hour.

2. Preheat a browning dish according to the manufacturer's instructions. Brush lightly with oil and immediately add the cutlets, pressing down well so that they brown on the underside.

3. Microwave on HIGH for 1 minute, turn over and microwave on HIGH for a further 30-45 seconds, or until cooked.

4. Allow to stand for 2 minutes before removing from the dish with a slotted spoon. Serve hot or cold with a seasonal salad or vegetables.

## Two

1. Mix the cashews with the walnuts, shallot, breadcrumbs, spices, parsley, egg and salt and pepper to taste, mixing well. Divide and shape the mixture into 4 rounds or cutlet shapes, cover and chill for at least 1 hour.

2. Preheat a browning dish according to the manufacturer's instructions. Brush lightly with oil and immediately add the cutlets, pressing down well so that they brown on the underside.

3. Microwave on HIGH for 2 minutes, turn over and microwave on HIGH for a further 1-1½ minutes, or until cooked.

4. Allow to stand for 2 minutes before removing from the dish with a slotted spoon. Serve hot or cold with a seasonal salad or vegetables.

# *Butter Bean and Mushroom Bourguignonne*

Remember to start this dish the day before you want it by soaking the butter beans overnight in cold water. Should you forget then hasten the soaking process by placing the beans in a dish and covering with boiling water, covering the dish and cooking on HIGH for 5 minutes, then leaving to stand for just 1½ hours before using.

| One | | Two |
|---|---|---|
| 100 g/4 oz | dried butter beans, soaked overnight in cold water | 225 g/8 oz |
| | boiling water to cover | |
| ½ | onion, peeled and chopped | 1 |
| ½ | clove of garlic, crushed | 1 |
| 225g/8 oz | ripe tomatoes, skinned and sliced | 450 g/1 lb |
| 1 small | bay leaf | 1 |
| 2.5 ml/½ tsp | chopped mixed fresh herbs | 5 ml/1 tsp |
| 150 ml/¼ pt | red wine | 300 ml/½ pt |
| 15 ml/1 tbsp | tomato paste | 30 ml/2 tbsp |
| | salt and pepper | |
| 50 g/2 oz | mushrooms, wiped and sliced | 100 g/4 oz |
| 15 ml/1 tbsp | chopped parsley | 30 ml/2 tbsp |

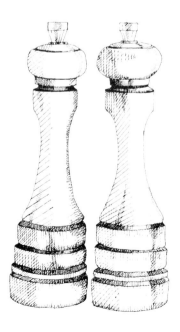

*Honey and Mustard Basted Vegetable Kebabs (page 83) and Wild-Rice Salad Bowl with Feta and Hazlenuts (page 79)*

## One

1. Rinse and drain the beans and place in a medium dish with sufficient boiling water to cover. Microwave on HIGH for 10 minutes, stirring once. Leave to stand, covered, while preparing the sauce.

2. Place the onion and garlic in a medium dish, cover and microwave on HIGH for 2 minutes, stirring once.

3. Add the tomatoes, herbs, wine, tomato paste and salt and pepper to taste, mixing well. Cover and microwave on HIGH for 7 minutes, stirring once.

4. Drain the butter beans and add to the tomato mixture. Cover and microwave on HIGH for 7 minutes, then reduce the power setting to MEDIUM and microwave for a further 15-20 minutes, or until the beans are tender, stirring twice.

5. Add the mushrooms and parsley and microwave on MEDIUM for a further 3-4 minutes. Serve hot.

## Two

1. Rinse and drain the beans and place in a medium dish with sufficient boiling water to cover. Microwave on HIGH for 10 minutes, stirring once. Leave to stand, covered, while preparing the sauce.

2. Place the onion and garlic in a large dish, cover and microwave on HIGH for 3 minutes, stirring once.

3. Add the tomatoes, herbs, wine, tomato paste and salt and pepper to taste, mixing well. Cover and microwave on HIGH for 10 minutes, stirring once.

4. Drain the butter beans and add to the tomato mixture. Cover and microwave on HIGH for 10 minutes, then reduce the power setting to MEDIUM and microwave for a further 20 minutes, or until the beans are tender, stirring twice.

5. Add the mushrooms and parsley and microwave on MEDIUM for a further 5 minutes. Serve hot.

*Baby Vegetables and Tofu with Thai-Style Sauce, front (page 77) and Green Vegetables with Oriental Drizzle, back (page 78).*

# Baby Vegetables and Tofu with Thai-Style Sauce

It is easy to buy a good selection of baby vegetables from most supermarkets today to produce a colourful dish with a variety of textures and flavours. The selection below works well when combined with tofu and a powerful and flavoursome Thai sauce.

| One | | Two |
|---|---|---|
| ½ | clove of garlic, crushed | 1 |
| 7.5 ml/1½ tsp | finely chopped root ginger | 15 ml/1 tbsp |
| ½ | red chilli, seeded | 1 |
| 5 ml/1 tsp | snipped lemon grass | 10 ml/2 tsp |
| 1.25 ml/¼ tsp | Chinese 5-spice powder | 2.5 ml/½ tsp |
| 22.5 ml/1½ tbsp | coarsely chopped coriander | 45 ml/3 tbsp |
| 2 | spring onions, chopped | 4 |
| 5 ml/1 tsp | lime juice | 10 ml/2 tsp |
| 15 ml/1 tbsp | grapeseed or sunflower oil | 30 ml/2 tbsp |
| 40 g/1½ oz | dwarf corn | 75 g/3 oz |
| 25 g/1 oz | mangetout, trimmed | 50 g/2 oz |
| 2 | baby patty pan squash | 4 |
| 3 | baby asparagus spears | 6 |
| ½ | red pepper, cored, seeded and cubed | 1 |
| 150 ml/¼ pt | coconut milk | 300 ml/½ pt |
| 7.5 ml/1½ tsp | crunchy peanut butter | 15 ml/1 tbsp |
| 75 g/3 oz | firm tofu, cubed | 175 g/6 oz |
| | salt and pepper | |
| | sprigs of fresh coriander, to garnish | |

## One

1. Place the garlic, ginger, chilli, lemon grass, Chinese 5-spice powder, coriander, spring onions and lime juice in a blender and process until smooth.

2. Place the oil in a large bowl, add the herb and spice mixture and microwave, uncovered, on HIGH for 45 seconds.

3. Stir in the dwarf corn, mangetout, squash, asparagus, red pepper, coconut milk and peanut butter. Cover and microwave on HIGH for 3-4 minutes or until the vegetables are tender but still crisp, stirring once halfway through the cooking time.

4. Stir in the tofu and salt and pepper to taste. Cover and microwave on HIGH for a further 1½-2 minutes. Leave to stand for 1 minute before serving garnished with coriander sprigs. Serve with a rice or noodle accompaniment.

## Two

1. Place the garlic, ginger, chilli, lemon grass, Chinese 5-spice powder, coriander, spring onions and lime juice in a blender and process until smooth.

2. Place the oil in a large bowl, add the herb and spice mixture and microwave, uncovered, on HIGH for 1 minute.

3. Stir in the dwarf corn, mangetout, squash, asparagus, red pepper, coconut milk and peanut butter. Cover and microwave on HIGH for 6 minutes or until the vegetables are tender but still crisp, stirring once halfway through the cooking time.

4. Stir in the tofu and salt and pepper to taste. Cover and microwave on HIGH for a further 3 minutes. Leave to stand for 1 minute before serving garnished with coriander sprigs. Serve with a rice or noodle accompaniment.

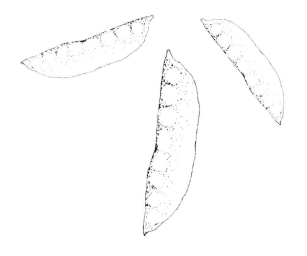

# Green Vegetables with Oriental Drizzle

Jewelled green vegetables when drizzled with special oriental seasonings make a special main-meal dish perfect for serving with rice.

| One | | Two |
|---|---|---|
| ½ | green pepper, cored, seeded and cut into strips | 1 |
| 50 g/2 oz | mangetout, trimmed | 100 g/4 oz |
| 3 | spring onions, trimmed and cut into bite-sized pieces | 6 |
| 50 g/2 oz | courgettes, thickly sliced | 100 g/4 oz |
| 7 g/¼ oz | fresh coriander, coarsely chopped | 15 g/½ oz |
| 3 | thin slices root ginger, peeled and cut into thin julienne | 6 |
| 15 ml/1 tbsp | tamari soy sauce | 30 ml/2 tbsp |
| 5 ml/1 tsp | vegetable oil | 10 ml/2 tsp |
| 10 ml/2 tsp | rice wine vinegar | 20 ml/4 tsp |

## One

1. Mix the green pepper with the mangetout, spring onions, courgettes, coriander, ginger, soy sauce, oil and rice wine vinegar in a medium dish, blending well.

2. Cover tightly and microwave on HIGH for 4 minutes, stirring once halfway through the cooking time.

3. Leave to stand, covered, for 1 minute before stirring to serve. Serve with cooked rice or noodles.

## Two

1. Mix the green pepper with the mangetout, spring onions, courgettes, coriander, ginger, soy sauce, oil and rice wine vinegar in a large dish, blending well.

2. Cover tightly and microwave on HIGH for 6 minutes, stirring once halfway through the cooking time.

3. Leave to stand, covered, for 1-2 minutes before stirring to serve. Serve with cooked rice or noodles.

# Wild-Rice Salad Bowl with Feta and Hazelnuts

Use a wild rice and white rice mixture for making this salad. There will be little time saving over conventional cooking but once prepared the rice needs little attention during cooking.

| One | | Two |
|---|---|---|
| 50 g/2 oz | white and wild rice mix | 100 g/4 oz |
| 100 ml/3½ fl oz | boiling water | 200 ml/7 fl oz |
| | small knob of butter | |
| 2.5-cm/1-inch | piece of cucumber, chopped | 5-cm/2-inch |
| 1 | tomatoes, sliced | 2 |
| 2 | spring onions, chopped | 4 |
| ¼ | red pepper, cored, seeded and sliced | ½ |
| ¼ | green pepper, cored, seeded and sliced | ½ |
| 25 g/1 oz | vegetarian feta cheese, crumbled | 50 g/2 oz |
| 25 g/1 oz | toasted hazelnuts, coarsely chopped | 50 g/2 oz |
| | Dressing: | |
| 15 ml/1 tbsp | extra-virgin olive oil | 30 ml/2 tbsp |
| 10 ml/2 tsp | lemon juice | 20 ml/4 tsp |
| ½ | clove of garlic, crushed | 1 |
| 7.5 ml/1½ tsp | chopped fresh mint | 15 ml/1 tbsp |
| 7.5 ml/1½ tsp | chopped fresh chervil | 15 ml/1 tbsp |
| | salt and pepper | |

## One and Two

1. Place the rice mix in a bowl and pour over the boiling water. Add the knob of butter and stir well to melt. Cover and microwave on HIGH for 3 minutes. Reduce the power setting to MEDIUM and microwave for a further 12 minutes, stirring twice. Add a little more boiling water if the mixture cooks too dry. Leave to stand, covered, for 5 minutes before draining and refreshing under cold running water.

2. Place the cucumber, tomatoes, spring onions, peppers, cheese and hazelnuts in a salad bowl. Add the cooled cooked rice mixture.

3. To make the dressing, beat the oil with the lemon juice, garlic, mint, chervil and salt and pepper to taste, blending well.

4. Drizzle over the rice mixture and toss gently to coat. Serve as soon as possible.

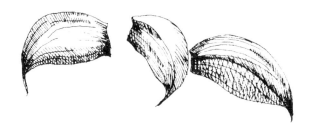

# Millet-Stuffed Peppers with Yellow Pepper Sauce

I use red peppers for holding the savoury millet stuffing in this recipe, the colour contrasts beautifully with the vibrant yellow pepper sauce with which they are served. You can of course vary the pepper colour using green peppers for the stuffing and red peppers for the sauce for example.

| One | | Two |
|---|---|---|
| 1 | medium red peppers | 2 |
| 15 ml/1 tbsp | water | 30 ml/2 tbsp |
| | Stuffing: | |
| 7.5 ml/1½ tsp | olive oil | 15 ml/1 tbsp |
| ¼ | onion, peeled and chopped | ½ |
| ½ | clove of garlic, crushed | 1 |
| 40 g/1½ oz | millet | 75 g/3 oz |
| 125 ml/4 fl oz | hot vegetable stock or boiling water | 250 ml/8 fl oz |
| ½ | medium courgette, grated | 1 |
| 25 g/1 oz | mushrooms, chopped | 50 g/2 oz |
| 10 ml/2 tsp | chopped fresh parsley | 20 ml/4 tsp |
| | salt and pepper | |
| | Sauce: | |
| ½ | yellow pepper, cored, seeded and chopped | 1 |
| 15 ml/1 tbsp | water | 30 ml/2 tbsp |
| 37.5 ml/2½ tbsp | natural yogurt | 75 ml/5 tbsp |
| | dash of Tabasco sauce flat-leaf parsley | |
| | sprigs, to garnish | |

VEGETARIAN MICROWAVE COOKING FOR ONE & TWO

# One

1. Halve the red pepper lengthways, remove and discard the core and seeds and place in a medium shallow dish with the water. Cover and microwave on HIGH for 4-5 minutes, rearranging once, until the pepper halves are tender. Allow to cool.

2. Meanwhile, place the oil in a medium bowl with the onion and garlic. Cover and microwave on HIGH for 1½ minutes until softened. Remove half of the mixture with a slotted spoon and set aside for the sauce.

3. Add the millet to the remaining onion and garlic mixture with the stock or water. Cover loosely and microwave on HIGH for 3 minutes. Reduce the power setting to MEDIUM and microwave for a further 12 minutes, stirring twice until the millet grains are tender. Add the grated courgette and mushrooms, re-cover and leave to stand for 3 minutes.

4. Add the parsley and salt and pepper to the millet and mix well. Use this mixture to stuff the red pepper halves and place in a heatproof dish.

5. Meanwhile, to make the sauce, place the yellow pepper in a bowl with the water, cover and microwave on HIGH for 1-2 minutes until very soft. Drain thoroughly. Place in a blender with the reserved onion mixture, yogurt, Tabasco sauce and salt and pepper to taste. Purée until smooth.

6. Cover the peppers and microwave on HIGH for 2-2½ minutes or until hot and tender. Transfer to a serving plate and surround with a pool of the warm yellow pepper sauce. Garnish with flat-leaf parsley sprigs and serve at once.

# Two

1. Halve the red peppers lengthways, remove and discard the cores and seeds and place in a large shallow dish with the water. Cover and microwave on HIGH for 6-8 minutes, rearranging once, until the pepper halves are tender. Allow to cool.

2. Meanwhile, place the oil in a medium bowl with the onion and garlic. Cover and microwave on HIGH for 1½-2 minutes until softened. Remove half of the mixture with a slotted spoon and set aside for the sauce.

3. Add the millet to the remaining onion and garlic mixture with the stock or water. Cover loosely and microwave on HIGH for 3 minutes. Reduce the power setting to MEDIUM and microwave for a further 12 minutes, stirring twice until the millet grains are tender. Add the grated courgette and mushrooms, re-cover and leave to stand for 3 minutes.

4. Add the parsley and salt and pepper to the millet and mix well. Use this mixture to stuff the red pepper halves and place in a heatproof dish.

5. Meanwhile, to make the sauce, place the yellow pepper in a bowl with the water, cover and microwave on HIGH for 1½-2½ minutes until very soft. Drain thoroughly. Place in a blender with the reserved onion mixture, yogurt, Tabasco sauce and salt and pepper to taste. Purée until smooth.

6. Cover the peppers and microwave on HIGH for 3-4 minutes or until hot and tender. Transfer to two individual serving plates and surround with pools of the warm yellow pepper sauce. Garnish with flat-leaf parsley sprigs and serve at once.

*80*

# *Rainbow Rice and Vegetable Salad with Raspberry Dressing*

Serve this salad as either a light appetiser, salad course or with a protein-based dish as a main course. For added crunch you might like to add a few fried rice sticks to the rainbow mixture. Either sprinkle over the arranged salad or add to the salad bowl mixture and toss lightly to avoid crushing the crisp sticks.

| One | | Two |
| --- | --- | --- |
| 50 g/2 oz | long-grain white rice | 100 g/4 oz |
| 150 ml/¼ pt | boiling water | 300 ml/½ pt |
| | salt and pepper | |
| 50 g/2 oz | spinach leaves | 100 g/4 oz |
| ¼ | small head of radicchio | ½ |
| 25 g/1 oz | shiitake mushrooms, sliced | 50 g/2 oz |
| ¼ | red pepper, cored, seeded and cut into julienne | ½ |
| ¼ | yellow pepper, cored, and cut into julienne | ½ |
| | Dressing: | |
| 3.75 ml/¾ tsp | finely grated fresh root ginger | 7.5 ml/1½ tsp |
| 1.25 ml/¼ tsp | grated orange zest | 2.5 ml/½ tsp |
| 10 ml/2 tsp | raspberry vinegar | 20 ml/4 tsp |
| 7.5 ml/1½ tsp | safflower oil | 15 ml/1 tbsp |
| 7.5 ml/1½ tsp | ginger juice or ginger wine | 15 ml/1 tbsp |
| 0.6 ml/⅛ tsp | Chinese chilli sauce | 1.25 ml/¼ tsp |

## One and Two

1. Place the rice in a medium bowl and pour over the boiling water. Add a pinch of salt, cover loosely and microwave on HIGH for 3 minutes. Reduce the power setting to MEDIUM and microwave for a further 12 minutes, stirring twice. Leave to stand, covered, for 3 minutes before draining and rinsing under cold water.

2. Meanwhile, thinly shred the spinach and radicchio leaves. Either arrange in rows on a serving plate with the mushrooms, peppers and rice or place in a medium bowl.

3. To make the dressing, beat the ginger with the orange zest, raspberry vinegar, oil, ginger juice or wine, chilli sauce and salt and pepper to taste. Drizzle over the arranged salad to serve or add to the salad bowl and toss gently to coat for serving.

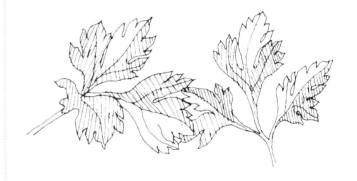

# Vegetable and Chestnut Casserole

This is a wonderful casserole to serve during the autumn and winter months; use fresh, shelled chestnuts when available and dried when not. If using dried, then speed up the rehydration process in the microwave about an hour before using.

| One | | Two |
|---|---|---|
| 100 g/4 oz | fresh chestnuts, shelled | 225 g/8 oz |
| | OR | |
| 50 g/2 oz | dried chestnuts | 100 g/4 oz |
| | boiling water | |
| 7.5 ml/1½ tsp | sunflower oil | 15 ml/1 tbsp |
| ½ | small leek, trimmed and finely sliced | 1 |
| ½ | carrot, peeled and cut into julienne | 1 |
| ½ | stick of celery, chopped | 1 |
| ¼ | red pepper, cored, seeded and sliced | ½ |
| | small piece of root ginger, peeled and grated | |
| | small bay leaf | |
| | pinch of grated nutmeg | |
| 7 g/¼ oz | wholemeal flour | 15 g/½ oz |
| 75 ml/5 tbsp | hot vegetable stock | 150 ml/¼ pt |
| 37.5 ml/2½ tbsp | red wine | 75 ml/5 tbsp |
| 1.25 ml/¼ tsp | demerara sugar | 2.5 ml/½ tsp |
| 7.5 ml/1½ tsp | tamari or soy sauce | 15 ml/1 tbsp |
| | salt and pepper | |
| | chopped fresh parsley, to garnish | |

## One

1. Place the dried chestnuts, if using, in a dish and add sufficient boiling water to cover. Cover and microwave on HIGH for 6 minutes, stirring once. Leave to stand, covered, for about 1 hour, then drain thoroughly to use.

2. Place the oil in a medium dish and microwave on HIGH for 45 seconds. Add the leek, carrot, celery, pepper, ginger, bay leaf and nutmeg, mixing well.

Cover and microwave on HIGH for 2 minutes, stirring once.

3. Stir in the flour and gradually add the stock and wine, blending well. Microwave, uncovered, for 1-1½ minutes or until boiling, stirring twice.

4. Add the chestnuts, sugar, tamari or soy sauce and salt and pepper to taste, mixing well. Cover and microwave on MEDIUM for 15-20 minutes, or until the chestnuts are soft and tender but not fallen.

5. Serve hot, sprinkled with chopped parsley. Accompany with potatoes, rice or pasta.

## Two

1. Place the dried chestnuts, if using, in a dish and add sufficient boiling water to cover. Cover and microwave on HIGH for 6 minutes, stirring once. Leave to stand, covered, for about 1 hour, then drain thoroughly to use.

2. Place the oil in a large dish and microwave on HIGH for 1½ minutes. Add the leek, carrot, celery, pepper, ginger, bay leaf and nutmeg, mixing well. Cover and microwave on HIGH for 4 minutes, stirring once.

3. Stir in the flour and gradually add the stock and wine, blending well. Microwave, uncovered, for 2-3 minutes or until boiling, stirring twice.

4. Add the chestnuts, sugar, tamari or soy sauce and salt and pepper to taste, mixing well. Cover and microwave on MEDIUM for 15-20 minutes, or until the chestnuts are soft and tender but not fallen.

5. Serve hot, sprinkled with the chopped parsley. Accompany with potatoes, rice or pasta.

# Honey and Mustard Basted Vegetable Kebabs

These very colourful vegetable kebabs are first marinated in a honey and mustard mixture to make them extra flavourful. Serve with rice and a crisp salad for a nutritious main meal. Remember to use plain cooked beetroot, not the type cooked then soaked in vinegar, for best results.

| One | | Two |
|---|---|---|
| 15 ml/1 tbsp | olive oil | 30 ml/2 tbsp |
| 7.5 ml/1½ tsp | lemon juice | 15 ml/1 tbsp |
| 2.5 ml/½ tsp | honey | 5 ml/1 tsp |
| 2.5 ml/½ tsp | snipped chives | 5 ml/1 tsp |
| 2.5 ml/½ tsp | chopped parsley | 5 ml/1 tsp |
| 1.25 ml/¼ tsp | wholegrain mustard | 2.5 ml/½ tsp |
| | salt and pepper | |
| 2 | cauliflower florets | 4 |
| ½ | courgette, cut into thick rounds | 1 |
| 2 | shallots, peeled | 4 |
| 2 | small broccoli florets | 4 |
| 2 | cherry tomatoes | 4 |
| 2 | cooked baby beetroots | 4 |

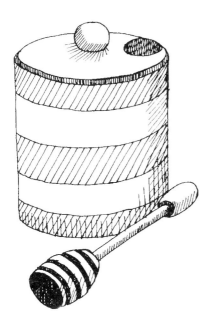

## One

1. Mix the oil with the lemon juice, honey, chives, parsley, mustard and salt and pepper to taste, mixing well. Add all the vegetables to the mixture except the beetroot, mixing well to coat. Cover and leave to stand for 1 hour, mixing occasionally.

2. Drain the vegetables and thread alternately on to a long wooden skewer including the beetroot but omitting the cherry tomatoes. Place on a microwave roasting rack or plate, brush with the marinade and microwave on HIGH for 2-2½ minutes, or until the vegetables are just tender. Turn the kebab over and brush again with the marinade.

3. Slide the tomatoes on to the ends of the skewer and brush with more marinade. Cover and microwave on HIGH for 30-45 seconds or until the tomatoes are just heated through. Serve on a bed of rice with a crisp salad accompaniment.

## Two

1. Mix the oil with the lemon juice, honey, chives, parsley, mustard and salt and pepper to taste, mixing well. Add all the vegetables to the mixture except the beetroot, mixing well to coat. Cover and leave to stand for 1 hour, mixing occasionally.

2. Drain the vegetables and thread alternately on to two long wooden skewers including the beetroot but omitting the cherry tomatoes. Place on a microwave roasting rack or plate, brush with the marinade and microwave on HIGH for 4-4½ minutes, or until the vegetables are just tender. Turn the kebabs over and brush again with the marinade.

3. Slide the tomatoes on to the ends of the skewers and brush with more marinade. Cover and microwave on HIGH for 2 minutes or until the tomatoes are just heated through. Serve on a bed of rice with a crisp salad accompaniment.

# Kitchen Garden and Cashew au Gratin

This tasty carrot, courgette, mushroom and cashew nut main meal dish is delicious served with baby new potatoes and a crisp green salad. Serving sizes are generous and will stretch to serve up to 3 with accompaniments.

| One | | Two |
|---|---|---|
| 225 g/8 oz | baby carrots, scrubbed | 450 g/1 lb |
| 40 ml/8 tsp | water | 75 ml/5 tbsp |
| 175 g/6 oz | courgettes, sliced | 350 g/12 oz |
| 50 g/2 oz | mushrooms, wiped and sliced | 100 g/4 oz |
| 100 g/4 oz | cashew nuts | 225 g/8 oz |
| 50 g/2 oz | vegetarian Cheddar cheese, grated | 100 g/4 oz |
| 15 g/½ oz | butter or margarine | 25 g/1 oz |
| 15 g/½ oz | plain flour | 25 g/1 oz |
| 150 ml/¼ pt | milk | 300 ml/½ pt |
| | soy sauce, to taste | |
| | salt and pepper | |
| 25 g/1 oz | wholemeal breadcrumbs | 50 g/2 oz |
| 25 g/1 oz | Parmesan cheese, grated | 50 g/2 oz |

## One

1. Place the carrots in a bowl with 30 ml/6 tsp of the water. Cover and microwave on HIGH for 8 minutes, stirring once. Drain thoroughly and set aside.

2. Place the courgettes a in bowl with the remaining 10 ml/2 tsp water. Cover and microwave on HIGH for 3 minutes, stirring once. Add the mushrooms and microwave on HIGH for a further 30 seconds. Drain thoroughly.

3. Mix the cooked vegetables with the nuts and the grated Cheddar cheese and place in a lightly buttered gratin dish.

4. To make the sauce, place the butter in a medium-sized jug and microwave on HIGH for 15-30 seconds to melt. Stir in the flour, then gradually add the milk. Microwave on HIGH for 2-2½ minutes, whisking every 1 minute until the sauce is smooth, boiling and thickened. Season with soy sauce, salt and pepper to taste. Pour the sauce over the vegetable and nut mixture.

5. Mix the breadcrumbs with the grated Parmesan cheese and sprinkle over the top of the sauce. Microwave on HIGH for 3-4 minutes, until the vegetables are tender and the sauce is hot. Brown quickly under a preheated hot grill until crisp and golden if you like. Serve hot.

## Two

1. Place the carrots in a bowl with 30 ml/6 tsp of the water. Cover and microwave on HIGH for 8 minutes, stirring once. Drain thoroughly and set aside.

2. Place the courgettes in a bowl with the remaining 10 ml/2 tsp water. Cover and microwave on HIGH for 3 minutes, stirring once. Add the mushrooms and microwave on HIGH for a further 30 seconds. Drain thoroughly.

3. Mix the cooked vegetables with the nuts and the grated Cheddar cheese and place in a lightly buttered gratin dish.

4. To make the sauce, place the butter in a medium-sized jug and microwave on HIGH for 15-30 seconds to melt. Stir in the flour, then gradually add the milk. Microwave on HIGH for 3½-4 minutes, whisking every 1 minute until the sauce is smooth, boiling and thickened. Season with soy sauce, salt and pepper to taste. Pour the sauce over the vegetable and nut mixture.

5. Mix the breadcrumbs with the grated Parmesan cheese and sprinkle over the top of the sauce. Microwave on HIGH for 5-7 minutes, until the vegetables are tender and the sauce is hot. Brown quickly under a preheated hot grill until crisp and golden if you like. Serve hot.

# VEGETABLES, SALADS AND SIDE DISHES

## Microwave Roasted Garlic

This isn't a dish for the faint-hearted but rather for those who are adventurous and certainly love garlic. The garlic is eaten rather like artichoke leaves between the teeth - the cooked garlic is surprisingly mild and nutty. Alternatively squeeze from the cloves on to toasted warm bread. A super, if unusual, starter for good friends to share or for one to indulge in on a quiet night.

| One | | Two |
| --- | --- | --- |
| 1 | heads of garlic | 2 |
| 30 ml/2 tbsp | vegetable stock | 60 ml/4 tbsp |
| 15 ml/1 tbsp | extra virgin olive oil | 30 ml/2 tbsp |

## One

1. Slice across the top of the whole head of garlic near to the top to reveal the cut cloves but still leaving the whole head intact. Place in a small bowl or measuring jug.

2. Mix the stock with the oil and pour over the garlic head. Tightly cover and microwave on HIGH for 3-3 ½ minutes, depending upon the size of the garlic head. Leave to stand for 5-10 minutes before serving.

## Two

1. Slice across the tops of the whole heads of garlic near to the top to reveal the cut cloves but still leaving the whole heads intact. Place in a medium bowl or measuring jug.

2. Mix the stock with the oil and pour over the garlic heads. Tightly cover and microwave on HIGH for 5 minutes. Leave to stand for 5-10 minutes before serving.

# Carrots in Soured Cream with Chives

Carrots make a colourful, if familiar, vegetable accompaniment to almost any meal but when mixed with soured cream, chives and spring onions have a luxurious quality all their own.

| One | | Two |
|---|---|---|
| 75 g/3 oz | carrots, peeled and cut into julienne strips | 175 g/6 oz |
| 15 ml/1 tbsp | water | 30 ml/2 tbsp |
| 1 | spring onions, chopped | 2 |
| 15 ml/1 tbsp | soured cream | 30 ml/2 tbsp |
| 5 ml/1 tsp | snipped chives | 10 ml/2 tsp |
| | pinch of brown sugar (*optional*) | |
| | salt and pepper | |

## One

1. Place the carrots and the water in a small dish. Cover and microwave on HIGH for 2-3 minutes, or until tender but still crisp, stirring once. Drain thoroughly.

2. Stir in the spring onions, soured cream, chives, sugar if using and salt and pepper to taste, mixing well. Cover and microwave on HIGH for 15-30 seconds, or until just heated through. Leave to stand for 2-3 minutes before serving.

## Two

1. Place the carrots and the water in a small dish. Cover and microwave on HIGH for 4-6 minutes, or until tender but still crisp, stirring once. Drain thoroughly.

2. Stir in the spring onions, soured cream, chives, sugar if using and salt and pepper to taste, mixing well. Cover and microwave on HIGH for 30-45 seconds, or until just heated through. Leave to stand for 2-3 minutes before serving.

# Creamed Baby Carrots with Basil

Here is a very simple recipe for a smart and stylish vegetable dish to serve as a main course accompaniment. Remember to season liberally with salt and pepper before serving.

| One | | Two |
|---|---|---|
| 100 g/4 oz | baby carrots | 225 g/8 oz |
| 15 ml/1 tbsp | water | 30 ml/2 tbsp |
| | salt and pepper | |
| 15 ml/1 tbsp | double cream | 30 ml/2 tbsp |
| 10 ml/2 tsp | chopped fresh basil | 20 ml/4 tsp |

## One

1. Scrub the carrots well or peel thinly but leave whole. Place in a dish with the water. Cover and microwave on HIGH for 3-4 minutes, stirring once halfway through the cooking time. Leave to stand for 1-2 minutes, then drain thoroughly.

2. Season the carrots liberally with salt and pepper to taste, then stir in the cream and basil. Toss well to coat in the herb mixture.

3. Microwave on HIGH for a further 30 seconds, stir well and serve immediately.

## Two

1. Scrub the carrots well or peel thinly but leave whole. Place in a dish with the water. Cover and microwave on HIGH for 6-8 minutes, stirring once halfway through the cooking time. Allow to stand for 1-2 minutes, then drain thoroughly.

2. Season the carrots with salt and pepper to taste, then stir in the cream and basil. Toss well to coat in the herb mixture.

3. Microwave on HIGH for a further 30-45 seconds, stir well and serve immediately.

# *Curried Potatoes with Chick Peas*

This is a splendid accompaniment to a vegetable curry. The dish may be cooked well ahead and then reheated for serving if you like.

## One                                            Two

| One | | Two |
|---|---|---|
| 175 g/6 oz | potatoes, peeled and cut into 2.5-cm/1-inch pieces | 350 g/12 oz |
| 15 ml/1 tbsp | water | 30 ml/2 tbsp |
| 50 g/2 oz | cauliflower florets | 100 g/4 oz |
| 25 g/1 oz | baby French beans, trimmed and halved | 50 g/2 oz |
| 3.75 ml/¾ tsp | sunflower oil | 7.5 ml/1½ tsp |
| 2.5 ml/½ tsp | ground coriander | 5 ml/1 tsp |
| 1.25 ml/¼ tsp | ground cumin | 2.5 ml/½ tsp |
| 1.25 ml/¼ tsp | ground turmeric | 2.5 ml/½ tsp |
| 100 g/4 oz | chopped canned tomatoes | 200 g/7 oz |
| 100 g/4 oz | canned chick peas | 200 g/7 oz |
| 7.5 ml/1½ tsp | chopped fresh coriander | 15 ml/1 tbsp |
| | salt and pepper | |

## One

1. Place the potatoes in a medium bowl with the water. Cover and microwave on HIGH for about 4-4½ minutes or until almost tender, stirring once halfway through the cooking time.

2. Add the cauliflower florets and green beans, re-cover and microwave on HIGH for 1-1¼ minutes or until the vegetables are tender crisp. Drain well.

3. Place the oil and spices in a medium shallow dish and microwave on HIGH for 30 seconds. Stir in the cooked vegetables, tomatoes, chick peas and half of the coriander, mixing well.

4. Cover and microwave on HIGH for 1-1½ minutes, stirring once until the vegetables are tender and the chick pea sauce is hot and bubbly. Season to taste with salt and pepper and serve hot, sprinkled with the remaining fresh coriander.

## Two

1. Place the potatoes in a medium bowl with the water. Cover and microwave on HIGH for about 6-7 minutes or until almost tender, stirring once halfway through the cooking time.

2. Add the cauliflower florets and green beans, re-cover and microwave on HIGH for 2 minutes or until the vegetables are tender crisp. Drain well.

3. Place the oil and spices in a medium shallow dish and microwave on HIGH for 45 seconds. Stir in the cooked vegetables, tomatoes, chick peas and half of the coriander, mixing well.

4. Cover and microwave on HIGH for 2 minutes, stirring once until the vegetables are tender and the chick pea sauce is hot and bubbly. Season to taste with salt and pepper and serve hot, sprinkled with the remaining fresh coriander.

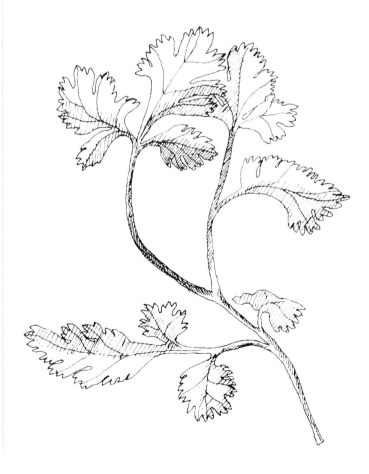

# *Peperonata*

Serve this traffic-light-coloured dish as a starter or as a vegetable accompaniment to a main meal. The dish is equally good served hot or cold.

## One       Two

| One | | Two |
|---|---|---|
| ½ | red pepper, cored and seeded | 1 |
| ½ | yellow pepper, cored and seeded | 1 |
| ½ | green pepper, cored and seeded | 1 |
| 15 ml/1 tbsp | olive oil | 30 ml/2 tbsp |
| ½ | large onion, peeled and finely sliced | 1 |
| | pinch of dried herbes de Provence | |
| ½ | clove of garlic, crushed | 1 |
| 100 g/4 oz | plum tomatoes, skinned, seeded and quartered lengthways | 225 g/8 oz |
| 7.5 ml/1½ tsp | balsamic vinegar | 15 ml/1 tbsp |
| 3 | black olives, halved and stoned | 5 |
| | salt and pepper | |

## One

1. Cut the peppers into large bite-sized pieces.

2. Place the oil in a medium bowl with the onion, herbs and garlic. Cover and microwave on HIGH for 2 minutes, until softened, stirring once halfway through the cooking time.

3. Add the peppers and tomatoes, mixing well. Cover and microwave on HIGH for 4-6 minutes until the peppers and tomatoes are well softened, stirring twice.

4. Add the vinegar, olives and salt and pepper to taste, mixing well. Serve warm or cold with crusty bread.

## Two

1. Cut the peppers into large bite-sized pieces.

2. Place the oil in a large bowl with the onion, herbs and garlic. Cover and microwave on HIGH for 3 minutes, until softened, stirring once halfway through the cooking time.

3. Add the peppers and tomatoes, mixing well. Cover and microwave on HIGH for 7-9 minutes until the peppers and tomatoes are well softened, stirring twice.

4. Add the vinegar, olives and salt and pepper to taste, mixing well. Serve warm or cold with crusty bread.

# *Spiced Julienne Parsnips*

This is the perfect parsnip dish to serve during the winter months with vegetable casseroles and nut roasts.

| One | | Two |
|---|---|---|
| 15 g/½ oz | butter | 25 g/1 oz |
| ¼ | onion, peeled and finely chopped | ½ |
| 100 g/4 oz | parsnips, peeled and cut into julienne strips | 225 g/8 oz |
| 10 ml/2 tsp | red wine | 20 ml/4 tsp |
| | small pinch of grated nutmeg | |
| | salt and pepper | |
| 5 ml/1 tsp | demerara sugar | 7.5 ml/1½ tsp |

## One

1. Place the butter in a small dish and microwave on HIGH for 30 seconds, or until melted.

2. Add the onion, mixing well. Cover and microwave on HIGH for ½-1 minute, until softened.

3. Add the parsnips, red wine, nutmeg and salt and pepper to taste, mixing well. Cover and microwave on HIGH for 3-5 minutes, until the parsnips are just tender but still crisp, stirring once halfway through the cooking time.

4. Stir in the sugar and serve at once.

## Two

1. Place the butter in a medium dish and microwave on HIGH for 45 seconds, or until melted.

2. Add the onion, mixing well. Cover and microwave on HIGH for 1-1½ minutes, until softened.

3. Add the parsnips, red wine, nutmeg and salt and pepper to taste, mixing well. Cover and microwave on HIGH for 5-7 minutes, until the parsnips are just tender but still crisp, stirring once halfway through the cooking time.

4. Stir in the sugar and serve at once.

# New Foodie Mash

Celeriac is hailed as the new 'mash' being served at umpteen smart city restaurants. This version made with a mixture of celeriac and potato has a slightly milder flavour but more versatile use. Serve as a vegetable accompaniment or as a topping for savoury vegetable mixtures.

| One | | Two |
|---|---|---|
| 100 g/4 oz | celeriac, peeled and cut into small cubes | 225 g/8 oz |
| 1 small | potato, peeled and cut into small cubes | 1 medium |
| 15 ml/1 tbsp | water | 30 ml/2 tbsp |
| 7.5 ml/1½ tsp | crème fraîche or natural yogurt | 15 ml/1 tbsp |
| 15 g/½ oz | butter | 25 g/1 oz |
| 5-10 ml/1-2 tsp | chopped fresh parsley | 10-15 ml/2-3 tsp |
| | salt and pepper | |

## One

1. Place the celeriac and potato cubes in a medium shallow dish with the water. Cover and microwave on HIGH for 6-7 minutes, or until tender, stirring every 2 minutes.

2. Drain thoroughly, then place in a food processor or blender with the crème fraîche or yogurt, butter, parsley and salt and pepper to taste and process until smooth. Alternatively, mash by hand until smooth and creamy.

3. Return to a serving dish and microwave on HIGH for about 1 minute until hot. Serve at once.

## Two

1. Place the celeriac and potato cubes in a large shallow dish with the water. Cover and microwave on HIGH for 8-10 minutes, or until tender, stirring every 3 minutes.

2. Drain thoroughly, then place in a food processor or blender with the crème fraîche or yogurt, butter, parsley and salt and pepper to taste and process until smooth. Alternatively, mash by hand until smooth and creamy.

3. Return to a serving dish and microwave on HIGH for 1-2 minutes until hot. Serve at once.

# Vegetable Ribbons

This colourful selection of julienne vegetables cooked with just a hint of herbs is perfect for serving with nut roasts, rissoles and burgers. The microwave ensures that the colours stay bright and that nutrients are saved.

## One                                                    Two

| One | | Two |
|---|---|---|
| 1 | medium courgettes, trimmed | 2 |
| 1 | medium carrots, peeled | 2 |
| ½ | red pepper, cored and seeded | 1 |
| ½ | yellow pepper, cored and seeded | 1 |
| 2 | spring onions, trimmed | 4 |
| 7 g/¼ oz | butter | 15 g/½ oz |
| 2.5 ml/½ tsp | chopped fresh mixed herbs (thyme, oregano and parsley for example) | 5 ml/1 tsp |
| 1.25 ml/¼ tsp | lemon juice | 2.5 ml/½ tsp |
| | salt and pepper | |

## One

1. Cut the courgettes, carrots, peppers and spring onions into julienne strips.

2. Place the butter in a medium bowl and microwave on HIGH for about 20 seconds, or until melted.

3. Add the prepared vegetables, herbs, lemon juice and salt and pepper to taste and mix well. Cover and microwave on HIGH for 2 minutes, or until the vegetables are tender but still crisp, stirring once halfway through the cooking time. Serve at once.

## Two

1. Cut the courgettes, carrots, peppers and spring onions into julienne strips.

2. Place the butter in a medium bowl and microwave on HIGH for 30 seconds, or until melted.

3. Add the prepared vegetables, herbs, lemon juice and salt and pepper to taste, mixing well. Cover and microwave on HIGH for 2½ - 3 minutes, or until the vegetables are tender but still crisp, stirring once halfway through the cooking time. Serve at once.

# Chinese-Style Vegetables with Cashew Nuts

Serve this ginger and soy-flavoured vegetable dish as part of a Chinese meal or as an unusual and flavoursome accompaniment to nut burgers and roasts.

## One                                                    Two

| One | | Two |
|---|---|---|
| 7.5 ml/1½ tsp | oil | 15 ml/1 tbsp |
| 5 ml/1 tsp | grated root ginger | 10 ml/2 tsp |
| | pinch of cayenne pepper | |
| | pinch of Chinese 5-spice powder | |
| 15 ml/1 tbsp | cashew nuts | 30 ml/2 tbsp |
| ½ | red pepper, cored, seeded and sliced | 1 |
| ½ small | onion, peeled and sliced | 1 small |
| 50 g/2 oz | fresh beansprouts | 100 g/4 oz |
| 50 g/2 oz | shiitake mushrooms, sliced or cut into pieces | 100 g/4 oz |
| 2.5 ml/½ tsp | soft brown sugar | 5 ml/1 tsp |
| 7.5 ml/1½ tsp | soy sauce | 15 ml/1 tbsp |
| | salt and pepper | |

## One

1. Place the oil, ginger, cayenne pepper, Chinese 5- spice powder and cashews in a medium bowl, mixing well. Microwave on HIGH for 2-3 minutes, or until lightly browned, stirring every 1 minute.

2. Remove the nuts from the dish with a slotted spoon and reserve.

3. Add the red pepper, onion, beansprouts, mushrooms, sugar, soy sauce and salt and pepper to taste to the dish juices and mix well. Microwave on HIGH for 2½-3 minutes, until the vegetables are tender but still crisp, stirring every 1 minute.

4. Stir in the reserved cashew nuts and serve at once.

## Two

1. Place the oil, ginger, cayenne pepper, Chinese 5-spice powder and cashew nuts in a medium bowl, mixing well. Microwave on HIGH for 3-4 minutes, until lightly browned, stirring every 1 minute.

2. Remove the nuts from the dish with a slotted spoon and reserve.

3. Add the red pepper, onion, beansprouts, mushrooms, sugar, soy sauce and salt and pepper to taste to the dish juices and mix well. Microwave on HIGH for 3-4 minutes, until the vegetables are tender but still crisp, stirring every 1 minute.

4. Stir in the reserved cashew nuts and serve at once.

## *Vegetables for One and Two*

I often make a dish of richly varied and colourful vegetables for a vegetarian meal by simply selecting cleaned and sliced vegetables from the salad counter at my local supermarket (I also do the same to make a mixed vegetable soup). The selection can be varied on a whim and while it may seem an expensive way of buying vegetables there is never any waste!

| One | | Two |
|---|---|---|
| 300 g/10 oz | mixed assorted, trimmed, peeled and sliced vegetables (carrots, green beans, broccoli florets, cauliflower florets, cherry tomatoes, mangetout, asparagus, mushrooms, courgettes and pepper for example) | 600 g/1¼ lb |
| 30 ml/2 tbsp | chopped mixed fresh herbs (parsley, chives, basil and dill for example) | 60 ml/4 tbsp |
| | salt and pepper | |
| 15 g/½ oz | butter (*optional*) | 25 g/1 oz |

## One

1. Arrange the vegetables in a large shallow dish (a flan dish is ideal) with the slower-cooking vegetables (carrots, green beans, broccoli, cauliflower, peas, mangetout and cherry tomatoes for example) to the outside of the dish and the quicker-cooking vegetables (asparagus, spring onions, mushrooms, courgettes and peppers for example) in the centre.

2. Sprinkle with the herbs, salt and pepper to taste and dot with the butter if used.

3. Cover tightly and microwave on HIGH for 5 minutes, until the vegetables are tender crisp. Allow to stand for 1 minute before serving.

## Two

1. Arrange the vegetables in a large shallow dish (a flan dish is ideal) with the slower-cooking vegetables (carrots, green beans, broccoli, cauliflower, peas, mangetout and cherry tomatoes for example) to the outside of the dish and the quicker-cooking vegetables (asparagus, spring onions, mushrooms, courgettes and peppers for example) in the centre.

2. Sprinkle with the herbs, salt and pepper to taste and dot with the butter if used.

3. Cover tightly and microwave on HIGH for 7-7½ minutes, until the vegetables are tender crisp. Allow to stand for 1 minute before serving.

# Autumn Apple and Aubergine Ratatouille

This is a tasty vegetable dish to make when windfall apples and plump shiny aubergines are at their best during the autumn months.

| One | | Two |
|---|---|---|
| ¼ | large onion, peeled and sliced | ½ |
| ¼ | red pepper, cored, seeded and sliced | ½ |
| 1 | courgettes, sliced | 2 |
| ¼ | medium aubergine, halved and sliced | ½ |
| 100 g/4 oz | cooking apples, peeled, cored and sliced | 225 g/8 oz |
| 1.25 ml/1¼ tsp | dried Herbes de Provence | 2.5 ml/½ tsp |
| | salt and pepper | |
| 100 g/4 oz | canned chopped tomatoes | 225 g/8 oz |

## One

1. Place the onion, pepper, courgette, aubergine, apple and herbs in a medium bowl. Cover tightly and microwave on HIGH for 3½ - 4 minutes, stirring once.

2. Season to taste with salt and pepper, then stir in the chopped tomatoes. Cover and microwave on HIGH for 3 - 3½ minutes, stirring once until tender.

3. Allow to stand, covered, for 2 minutes before serving.

## Two

1. Place the onion, pepper, courgettes, aubergine, apple and herbs in a large bowl. Cover tightly and microwave on HIGH for 7 - 8 minutes, stirring once.

2. Season to taste with salt and pepper, then stir in the chopped tomatoes. Cover and microwave on HIGH for 6 - 7 minutes, stirring once until tender.

3. Allow to stand, covered, for 2 minutes before serving.

# Gingered Red Cabbage with Pine Nuts

This is an aromatic, fruity red cabbage dish that makes a superb accompaniment to nut roasts. Try to use balsamic vinegar if possible but if not use a good quality red wine vinegar sweetened with a little muscovado sugar.

| One | | Two |
|---|---|---|
| 100 g/4 oz | red cabbage, very finely sliced | 225 g/8 oz |
| 5 ml/1 tsp | olive oil | 10 ml/2 tsp |
| 2.5 ml/½ tsp | grated fresh root ginger | 5 ml/1 tsp |
| 15 ml/1 tbsp | vegetable stock | 30 ml/2 tbsp |
| | salt and pepper | |
| 5 ml/1 tsp | balsamic vinegar | 10 ml/2 tsp |
| 5 ml/1 tsp | port wine or cranberry jelly | 10 ml/2 tsp |
| 7 g/¼ oz | toasted pine nuts | 15 g/½ oz |

## One

1. Place the red cabbage in a medium bowl with the oil and ginger. Microwave on HIGH for 2 minutes, stirring once.

2. Add the stock with salt and pepper to taste, mixing well. Cover tightly and microwave on HIGH for a further 3-4 minutes, stirring once, until the cabbage is tender. Allow to stand for 2 minutes.

3. Add the vinegar, jelly and pine nuts, mixing well. Taste and adjust the seasoning if necessary. Serve warm.

## Two

1. Place the red cabbage in a medium bowl with the oil and ginger. Microwave on HIGH for 3 minutes, stirring once.

2. Add the stock with salt and pepper to taste, mixing well. Cover tightly and microwave on HIGH for a further 4-6 minutes, stirring once, until the cabbage is tender. Allow to stand for 2 minutes.

3. Add the vinegar, jelly and pine nuts, mixing well. Taste and adjust the seasoning if necessary. Serve warm.

# Broccoli with Ginger and Sesame Seeds

Broccoli, cooked until tender, then tossed with a crisp ginger- and sesame-flavoured crumb mixture makes a wonderful vegetable accompaniment to a vegetarian main meal.

| One | | Two |
|---|---|---|
| 100 g/4 oz | broccoli spears | 225 g/8 oz |
| 15 ml/1 tbsp | water | 30 ml/2 tbsp |
| 15 g/½ oz | butter | 25 g/1 oz |
| ¼ | small onion, peeled and very finely chopped | ½ |
| 1.25 ml/¼ tsp | grated root ginger | 2.5 ml/½ tsp |
| 22.5 ml/1½ tbsp | fresh white breadcrumbs | 45 ml/3 tbsp |
| 7.5 ml/1½ tsp | sesame seeds | 15 ml/1 tbsp |

## One

1. Trim the broccoli and slice diagonally into 5-cm/2-inch pieces. Place in a shallow cooking dish with the water. Cover and microwave on HIGH for about 3 minutes until just tender but still crisp. Leave to stand, covered, while cooking the topping.

2. Place the butter in a large shallow dish with the onion and ginger. Cover and microwave on HIGH for about 1 minute, stirring once until the onion is just tender.

3. Stir in the breadcrumbs and microwave on HIGH for 1-2 minutes, stirring every 1 minute until the crumbs are crisp and golden.

4. Add the sesame seeds and mix well. Drain the broccoli throughly and place in a warmed serving dish. Sprinkle over the crumb mixture and toss gently to serve.

## Two

1. Trim the broccoli and slice diagonally into 5-cm/2-inch pieces. Place in a shallow cooking dish with the water. Cover and microwave on HIGH for about 4½-5 minutes until just tender but still crisp. Leave to stand, covered, while cooking the topping.

2. Place the butter in a large shallow dish with the onion and ginger. Cover and microwave on HIGH for about 1-1½ minutes, stirring once until the onion is just tender.

3. Stir in the breadcrumbs and microwave on HIGH for 1½-2½ minutes, stirring every 1 minute until the crumbs are crisp and golden.

4. Add the sesame seeds and mix well. Drain the broccoli thoroughly and place in a warmed serving dish. Sprinkle over the crumb mixture and toss gently to serve.

# Creamed Green Beans

This bean dish made of freshly cooked green beans tossed in a smooth creamy dressing spiked with a little mustard tastes equally good hot or cold.

| One | | Two |
| --- | --- | --- |
| 100 g/4 oz | fine green beans | 225 g/8 oz |
| 15 ml/1 tbsp | water | 30 ml/2 tbsp |
| 5 ml/1 tsp | mayonnaise | 10 ml/2 tsp |
| 5 ml/1 tsp | natural yogurt or plain fromage frais | 10 ml/2 tsp |
| 2.5 ml/½ tsp | wholegrain mustard | 5 ml/1 tsp |
| | salt and pepper | |

## One

1. Trim the beans and place in a small bowl with the water. Cover tightly and microwave on HIGH for 2-3 minutes, stirring once halfway through the cooking time, until just tender but still crisp. Leave to stand, covered, for 2 minutes, then drain thoroughly.

2. Meanwhile, mix the mayonnaise with the yogurt or fromage frais, mustard and salt and pepper to taste.

3. Mix the beans with the mayonnaise mixture, tossing well to coat. Serve warm or leave to cool and serve cold.

## Two

1. Trim the beans and place in a medium bowl with the water. Cover tightly and microwave on HIGH for 3-4 minutes, stirring once halfway through the cooking time, until just tender but still crisp. Leave to stand, covered, for 2 minutes, then drain thoroughly.

2. Meanwhile, mix the mayonnaise with the yogurt or fromage frais, mustard and salt and pepper to taste.

3. Mix the beans with the mayonnaise mixture, tossing well to coat. Serve warm or leave to cool and serve cold.

# Succotash

Succotash is a South American dish of sweetcorn and butter beans, perfect for serving as a main meal vegetable accompaniment.

| One | | Two |
| --- | --- | --- |
| 7.5 ml/1½ tsp | olive oil | 15 ml/1 tbsp |
| ¼ | onion, peeled and finely chopped | ½ |
| ½ | small stick of celery, chopped | 1 |
| 40 g/1½ oz | frozen peas, thawed | 75 g/3 oz |
| 40 g/1½ oz | frozen sweetcorn kernels, thawed | 75 g/3 oz |
| 40 g/1½ oz | canned butter beans | 75 g/3 oz |
| 37.5 ml/2½ tbsp | single cream | 75 ml/5 tbsp |
| 5 ml/1 tsp | chopped fresh parsley | 10 ml/2 tsp |
| | salt and pepper | |

## One

1. Place the oil in a medium dish with the onion and celery. Cover and microwave on HIGH for 45-60 seconds, stirring once.

2. Add the peas and sweetcorn, re-cover and microwave on HIGH for 1-1½ minutes, until just tender, stirring once.

3. Add the butter beans, cream, parsley and salt and pepper to taste, mixing well. Cover and microwave on HIGH for 30-60 seconds, until the mixture is hot, stirring once. **Do not allow the mixture to boil or the cream will separate.**

4. Serve hot as a vegetable accompaniment.

## Two

1. Place the oil in a medium dish with the onion and celery. Cover and microwave on HIGH for 1-1½ minutes, stirring once.

2. Add the peas and sweetcorn, re-cover and microwave on HIGH for 2-2½ minutes, until just tender, stirring once.

3. Add the butter beans, cream, parsley and salt and pepper to taste, mixing well. Cover and microwave on HIGH for 45-75 seconds, until the mixture is hot, stirring twice. **Do not allow the mixture to boil or the cream will separate.**

4. Serve hot as a vegetable accompaniment.

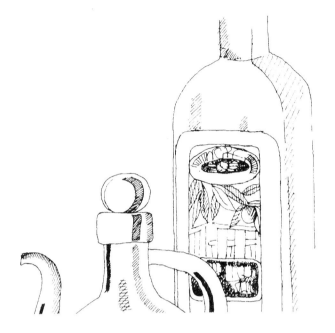

# Macque Choux

Macque Choux is a native American corn dish that was introduced to the Cajuns by local native Americans. It is simply freshly cooked corn kernels stepped up in flavour with green peppers, tomato and Tabasco sauce. Serve as a spicy vegetable accompaniment.

| One | | Two |
|---|---|---|
| 100 g/4 oz | **fresh husked sweetcorn kernels** | 225 g/8 oz |
| 30 ml/2 tbsp | water | 60 ml/4 tbsp |
| | small knob of butter | |
| ¼ | onion, peeled and chopped | ½ |
| ¼ | small green pepper, cored, seeded and chopped | ½ |
| ½ | tomato, skinned, seeded and chopped | 1 |
| | dash of Tabasco sauce | |
| | salt and pepper | |

## One

1. Place the sweetcorn kernels in a bowl with the water. Cover and microwave on HIGH for 3 minutes, stirring once. Drain thoroughly.

2. Add the butter, onion and green pepper, mixing well. Cover and microwave on HIGH for 1-1½ minutes, or until the corn and vegetables are tender crisp, stirring once.

3. Add the tomato, Tabasco and salt and pepper to taste, mixing well. Serve hot with rice and pasta dishes.

## Two

1. Place the sweetcorn kernels in a bowl with the water. Cover and microwave on HIGH for 4½-5 minutes, stirring once. Drain thoroughly.

2. Add the butter, onion and green pepper, mixing well. Cover and microwave on HIGH for a further 2-3 minutes, or until the corn and vegetables are tender crisp, stirring once.

3. Add the tomato, Tabasco and salt and pepper to taste, mixing well. Serve hot with rice and pasta dishes.

# Heat-of-the-Mid-Day-Sun Potatoes

Jacket potatoes make the ideal main-meal accompaniment but sometimes scream out for a spicy topping or dressing to give them a bit more interest. These potatoes with their tahini, chilli, coriander and sun-dried tomato topping have just that extra kick needed.

| One | | Two |
|---|---|---|
| 1 | baking potatoes, weighing about 225 g/8 oz | 2 |
| 60 g/2½ oz | tahini (sesame seed dressing) | 150 g/5 oz |
| 7.5 ml/1½ tsp | wholegrain mustard | 15 ml/1 tbsp |
| | pinch of chilli powder | |
| | pinch of onion powder | |
| 1 | sun-dried tomatoes in oil, very finely chopped | 2 |
| 7.5 ml/1½ tsp | chopped fresh coriander | 15 ml/1 tbsp |

## One

1. Scrub the potato, prick the skin with a fork and place on a double thickness sheet of absorbent kitchen paper and microwave on HIGH for 6-7 minutes, turning over once, until tender and soft to the squeeze. Wrap in foil and leave to stand while preparing the topping.

2. To make the filling, mix the tahini with the mustard, chilli powder, onion powder, sun-dried tomato and coriander.

3. Remove the potato from the foil and cut in half. Fork the flesh in the skins slightly and place on a warmed serving plate. Spoon over the prepared topping and serve at once.

## Two

1. Scrub the potatoes, prick the skins with a fork and place on a double thickness sheet of absorbent kitchen paper and microwave on HIGH for 10-12

minutes, turning over once, until tender and soft to the squeeze. Wrap in foil and leave to stand while preparing the topping.

2. To make the filling, mix the tahini with the mustard, chilli powder, onion powder, sun-dried tomatoes and coriander.

3. Remove the potatoes from the foil and cut each in half. Fork the flesh in the skins slightly and place on a warmed serving plate. Spoon over the prepared topping and serve at once.

# Easy Vegetable Gratin

This is the perfect vegetable accompaniment to make when using up small amounts of fresh vegetables. For best results flash under a preheated hot grill after microwave cooking.

| One | | Two |
|---|---|---|
| 25 g/1 oz | small broccoli florets | 50 g/2 oz |
| 25 g/1 oz | small cauliflower florets | 50 g/2 oz |
| 25 g/1 oz | mushrooms, wiped and sliced | 50 g/2 oz |
| 1 | small carrots, peeled and thinly sliced | 2 |
| ½ | small onion, peeled and chopped | 1 |
| 7.5 ml/1½ tsp | water | 15 ml/1 tbsp |
| 7 g/¼ oz | butter or margarine | 15 g/½ oz |
| 7.5 ml/1½ tsp | plain flour | 15 ml/1 tbsp |
| 37.5 ml/2½ tbsp | milk | 75 ml/5 tbsp |
| | salt and pepper | |
| 15 g/½ oz | vegetarian Cheddar cheese, grated | 25 g/1 oz |

## One

1. Place the broccoli, cauliflower, mushrooms, carrot, onion and water in a medium bowl. Cover and microwave on HIGH for 4 - 4½ minutes, stirring once, or until the vegetables are just tender crisp.

2. Place the butter or margarine in a jug with the flour and milk, mixing well. Microwave on HIGH for 1-1¼ minutes, beating twice, until smooth, boiling and thickened.

3. Add the sauce to the vegetables with salt and pepper to taste, mixing well. Spoon into a small flameproof dish and sprinkle with the cheese. Flash under a preheated hot grill until golden and bubbly, about 1-2 minutes. Serve hot.

## Two

1. Place the broccoli, cauliflower, mushrooms, carrots, onion and water in a medium bowl. Cover and microwave on HIGH for 4-6 minutes, stirring once, or until the vegetables are just tender crisp.

2. Place the butter or margarine in a jug with the flour and milk, mixing well. Microwave on HIGH for 1½-2 minutes, beating twice, until smooth, boiling and thickened.

3. Add the sauce to the vegetables with salt and pepper to taste, mixing well. Spoon into a medium flameproof dish and sprinkle with the cheese. Flash under a preheated hot grill until golden and bubbly, about 1-2 minutes. Serve hot.

# Traffic-Light Pepper Salad

This is a wonderfully colourful salad of peppers that is perfect to serve with crusty bread as a light starter. Serve warm or chilled, dusted with vegetarian Parmesan cheese, if you like.

| One | | Two |
|---|---|---|
| ½ | yellow pepper | 1 |
| ½ | green pepper | 1 |
| ½ | red pepper | 1 |
| 7.5 ml/1½ tsp | extra virgin olive oil | 15 ml/1 tbsp |
| 2.5 ml/½ tsp | fennel seeds | 5 ml/1 tsp |
| 1.25 ml/¼ tsp | dried oregano | 2.5 ml/½ tsp |
| 7.5 ml/1½ tsp | water | 15 ml/1 tbsp |
| | salt and pepper | |
| | vegetarian Parmesan cheese, grated to serve *(optional)* | |

## One

1. Halve the peppers, then remove the core and seeds. Using a sharp knife, slice the peppers into thin julienne strips and place in a small bowl.

2. Mix the oil with the fennel seeds, oregano, water and salt and pepper to taste and pour over the peppers. Cover tightly and microwave on HIGH for 4 minutes, stirring once halfway through the cooking time.

3. Allow to stand for 2 minutes before serving warm or cooling then chilling to serve cold. If you like, dust the top of the pepper salad with vegetarian Parmesan before serving. Accompany with crusty bread.

## Two

1. Halve the peppers, then remove the core and seeds. Using a sharp knife, slice the peppers into thin julienne strips and place in a medium bowl.

2. Mix the oil with the fennel seeds, oregano, water and salt and pepper to taste and pour over the peppers. Cover tightly and microwave on HIGH for 6 minutes, stirring twice during the cooking time.

3. Allow to stand for 2 minutes before serving warm or cooling then chilling to serve cold. If you like, dust the top of the pepper salad with vegetarian Parmesan before serving. Accompany with crusty bread.

# Sushi Rice Salad with Avocado

This is a wonderful rice salad with many of the flavours associated with Japanese cuisine. Add a little dry-roasted nori (Japanese seaweed) if you can get it.

## One                                                           Two

| One | | Two |
|---|---|---|
| 75 g/3 oz | long-grain rice | 175 g/6 oz |
| 200 ml/7 fl oz | boiling water | 400 ml/14 fl oz |
| | salt and pepper | |
| 22.5 ml/1½ tbsp | rice vinegar | 45 ml/3 tbsp |
| 15 g/½ oz | sugar | 25 g/1 oz |
| 5 ml/1 tsp | toasted sesame seeds | 10 ml/2 tsp |
| 11.25 ml/2¼ tsp | sunflower oil | 22.5 ml/4½ tsp |
| 7.5 ml/1½ tsp | finely chopped | 15 ml/1 tbsp |
| | pickled ginger | |
| 1 | spring onions, chopped | 2 |
| 1 | small carrots, grated | 2 |
| ¼ | small cucumber, finely chopped | ½ |
| ½ | avocado, peeled, stoned and finely sliced | 1 |
| | Dressing: | |
| 2.5 ml/½ tsp | wasabi (Japanese green horseradish powder) | 5 ml/1 tsp |
| 3.75 ml/¾ tsp | hot water | 7.5 ml/1½ tsp |
| 7.5 ml/1½ tsp | cold water | 15 ml/1 tbsp |
| 7.5 ml/1½ tsp | soy sauce | 15 ml/1 tbsp |
| 2.5 ml/½ tsp | ginger juice | 5 ml/1 tsp |
| | (squeezed from fresh root ginger) | |

## One

1. Place the rice in a cooking dish with the boiling water and a pinch of salt. Cover loosely and microwave on HIGH for 3 minutes. Reduce the power setting to MEDIUM and microwave for a further 12 minutes, stirring twice. Leave to stand, covered, for 5 minutes.

2. Meanwhile, place half of the rice vinegar, the sugar and a pinch of salt in a small bowl and microwave on HIGH for 15-20 seconds until hot. Stir well to dissolve the sugar. Stir into the rice mixture and allow to cool.

3. Add the remaining rice vinegar, sesame seeds, oil, ginger, spring onions, carrot and cucumber to the cool rice, mixing well.

4. To make the dressing, stir the wasabi powder into the hot water, then add the cold water, soy sauce and ginger juice.

5. Add the avocado to the rice mixture with pepper to taste and toss gently to mix. Spoon on to a serving plate and drizzle with the prepared dressing to serve.

## Two

1. Place the rice in a cooking dish with the boiling water and a pinch of salt. Cover loosely and microwave on HIGH for 3 minutes. Reduce the power setting to MEDIUM and microwave for a further 12 minutes, stirring twice. Leave to stand, covered, for 5 minutes.

2. Meanwhile, place half of the rice vinegar, the sugar and a pinch of salt in a small bowl and microwave on HIGH for about 30 seconds until hot. Stir well to dissolve the sugar. Stir into the rice mixture and allow to cool.

3. Add the remaining rice vinegar, sesame seeds, oil, ginger, spring onions, carrot and cucumber to the cool rice, mixing well.

4. To make the dressing, stir the wasabi powder into the hot water, then add the cold water, soy sauce and ginger juice.

5. Add the avocado to the rice mixture with pepper to taste and toss gently to mix. Spoon on to a serving plate and drizzle with the prepared dressing to serve.

# Sicilian Couscous Salad

Couscous is shaped like a grain but is actually a pasta made of semolina wheat. It makes a delicious salad when combined with classic ingredients from Sicily - olives, peppers, capers, currants and pine nuts.

| One | | Two |
|---|---|---|
| 125 ml/4 fl oz | water | 250 ml/8 fl oz |
| 15 g/½ oz | currants | 25 g/1 oz |
| | salt and pepper | |
| 15 ml/1 tbsp | extra-virgin olive oil | 30 ml/2 tbsp |
| 75 ml/3 fl oz | couscous | 175 ml/6 fl oz |
| 1 small | clove of garlic, crushed | 1 large |
| ¼ | small onion, peeled and finely chopped | ½ |
| 7.5 ml/1½ tsp | red wine vinegar | 15 ml/1 tbsp |
| 1 | small red peppers, roasted and chopped | 2 |
| 20 g/¾ oz | pimiento-stuffed green olives, finely sliced | 40 g/1½ oz |
| 7.5 ml/1½ tsp | drained capers | 15 ml/1 tbsp |
| 15 g/½ oz | toasted pine nuts | 25 g/1 oz |
| 15 ml/1 tbsp | chopped flat-leaf parsley | 30 ml/2 tbsp |

## One

1. Place the water, currants, pinch of salt and one-third of the oil in a medium bowl. Cover and microwave on HIGH for 1-2 minutes, or until the mixture boils. Stir in the couscous and leave to stand, covered, for 5 minutes to swell the grains.

2. Meanwhile, place the remaining oil in a bowl with the garlic and onion. Microwave on HIGH for 1-1½ minutes until softened.

3. Fluff the grains of couscous with a fork, then stir in the onion mixture with the vinegar, peppers, olives, capers, pine nuts, parsley and salt and pepper to taste, mixing well. Serve at room temperature.

## Two

1. Place the water, currants, pinch of salt and one-third of the oil in a medium bowl. Cover and microwave on HIGH for 2-3 minutes, or until the mixture boils. Stir in the couscous and leave to stand, covered, for 5 minutes to swell the grains.

2. Meanwhile, place the remaining oil in a bowl with the garlic and onion. Microwave on HIGH for 1½-2 minutes until softened.

3. Fluff the grains of couscous with a fork, then stir in the onion mixture with the vinegar, peppers, olives, capers, pine nuts, parsley and salt and pepper to taste, mixing well. Serve at room temperature.

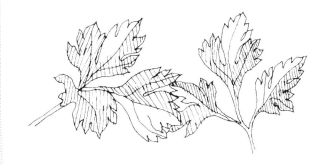

# Nutty Bulghur and Lentil Salad with Tarragon

Bulghur – wheat berries that have been steamed, dried and then cracked – can now be found in most supermarkets. When mixed with French green lentils and an aromatic tarragon-based dressing it makes a splendid starter or side dish.

| One | | Two |
|---|---|---|
| 50 g/2 oz | bulghur wheat | 100 g/4 oz |
| 125 ml/4 fl oz | boiling water | 250 ml/8 fl oz |
| | salt and pepper | |
| 50 g/2 oz | green lentils | 100 g/4 oz |
| 225 ml/7½ fl oz | hot vegetable stock | 450 ml/¾ pt |
| 1 | small shallots, peeled and finely chopped | 2 |
| 10 ml/2 tsp | tarragon vinegar | 20 ml/4 tsp |
| 1 | sticks celery, finely chopped | 2 |
| 1 | carrots, peeled and grated | 2 |
| 10 ml/2 tsp | finely chopped fresh tarragon | 20 ml/4 tsp |
| 10-15 ml/2-3 tsp | extra-virgin olive oil | 20-30 ml/4-6 tsp |
| 15 g/½ oz | walnuts, toasted and chopped | 25 g/1 oz |

## One and Two

1. Place the bulghur in a medium cooking dish with the water and a pinch of salt. Cover loosely and microwave on HIGH for 3 minutes. Reduce the power setting to MEDIUM and cook for 9-12 minutes, stirring twice during the cooking time. Leave to stand for 3-5 minutes, then fluff with a fork to separate the grains.

2. Meanwhile, place the lentils in a large bowl with the vegetable stock. Cover and microwave on HIGH for 20 minutes, stirring once, until the lentils are tender but still retain some bite. Drain thoroughly if necessary.

3. Mix the shallots with half of the tarragon vinegar and stir into the lentils, mixing well. Allow to cool, stirring occasionally.

4. Mix the lentils with the bulghur, celery, carrot and tarragon.

5. Beat the oil with the remaining tarragon vinegar and salt and pepper to taste. Stir into the lentil and bulghur mixture with the walnuts. Toss well and serve at room temperature.

# Sweet Potato Salad with Down-South Dressing

Sweet potatoes with their mealy, sweet-tasting texture cook wonderfully in the microwave. Slash and serve them topped with soured cream, mashed with seasonings or peeled and sliced in a salad with a zingy dressing like the one below.

| One | | Two |
|---|---|---|
| 1 x 250 g/9 oz | sweet potatoes | 2 x 250 g/9 oz |
| ½ | orange | 1 |
| 1 | spring onions | 2 |
| ¼ | green pepper | ½ |
| 1 | sticks celery | 2 |
| 15 g/½ oz | pecans or walnuts | 25 g/1 oz |
| 30 ml/2 tbsp | Down-South Dressing (see below) | 60 ml/4 tbsp |
| | salt and pepper | |

## One

1. Scrub the sweet potato and prick with a fork. Place on a double thickness sheet of absorbent kitchen paper and microwave on HIGH for 5-7 minutes, until tender, turning twice. Allow to cool for about 10 minutes.

*Sweet Potato Salad with Down-South Dressing, top (page 100) and Baby New Potatoes with Red Onion and Shredded Salad Leaves, bottom (page 101)*

2. Meanwhile, peel the orange removing any pith, then slice the flesh into bite-sized pieces. Trim the spring onion and chop finely. Core the pepper and cut into thin strips and finely slice the celery. Mix the orange flesh with the spring onion, pepper and celery, then crumble in the pecans or walnuts.

3. Carefully peel the skin away from the sweet potato, then cube or slice into the salad mixture while still warm.

4. Add the prepared dressing, season with salt and pepper to taste and toss gently to serve.

## Two

1. Scrub the sweet potatoes and prick with a fork. Place on a double thickness sheet of absorbent kitchen paper and microwave on HIGH for 8-10 minutes, until tender, turning twice. Allow to cool for about 10 minutes.

2. Meanwhile, peel the orange removing any pith, then slice the flesh into bite-sized pieces. Trim the spring onions and chop finely. Core the pepper and cut into thin strips and finely slice the celery. Mix the orange flesh with the spring onions, pepper and celery, then crumble in the pecans or walnuts.

3. Carefully peel the skin away from the sweet potatoes, then cube or slice into the salad mixture while still warm.

4. Add the prepared dressing, season with salt and pepper to taste and toss gently to serve.

## Down-South Dressing

Beat 50 ml/2 fl oz olive oil with 15 ml/1 tbsp red wine vinegar, 7.5 ml/1½ tsp wholegrain mustard, 15 ml/1 tbsp soft brown sugar and salt and pepper to taste. Delicious with potato-based salads.

*Smoked Tofu Kedgeree (page 65)*

# Baby New Potatoes with Red Onion and Shredded Salad Leaves

I love to prepare this dish when the very first baby Jersey new potatoes appear in early Spring. Expensive as they are, this special treatment with thinly sliced red onion and shredded new season salad leaves makes the outlay justifiable.

| One | | Two |
|---|---|---|
| 100 g/4 oz | baby new potatoes, scrubbed | 225 g/8 oz |
| 15 ml/1 tbsp | water | 30 ml/2 tbsp |
| 7.5 ml/1½ tsp | olive oil | 15 ml/1 tbsp |
| | OR | |
| 7 g/¼ oz | butter | 15 g/½ oz |
| ¼ | red onion, very thinly sliced | ½ |
| 25 g/1 oz | mixed salad leaves (lettuce, radicchio, rocket, frisée and lamb's lettuce for example), shredded | 50 g/2 oz |
| | salt and pepper | |

## One

1. Place the potatoes and the water in a bowl. Cover and microwave on HIGH for 3 minutes, stirring once. Leave to stand for 2 minutes, then drain thoroughly.

2. Return to the bowl, add the oil or butter and red onion, stirring well to mix. Cover and microwave on HIGH for 30-45 seconds.

3. Add the shredded salad leaves and salt and pepper to taste, mixing well. Serve at once.

## Two

1. Place the potatoes and the water in a bowl. Cover and microwave on HIGH for 6 minutes, stirring once. Leave to stand for 2 minutes, then drain thoroughly.

2. Return to the bowl, add the oil or butter and red onion, stirring well to mix. Cover and microwave on HIGH for 1 minute.

3. Add the shredded salad leaves and salt and pepper to taste, mixing well. Serve at once.

# Couscous, Orange and Cheese Salad

This is a light salad perfect for lunchtime eating. It can also be made with mandarin oranges either fresh or canned, but if using the latter make sure they are canned in fruit juice rather than syrup and add just 15-30 ml/1-2 tbsp of the juice to the yogurt dressing.

| One | | Two |
|---|---|---|
| 125 ml/4 fl oz | water | 250 ml/8 fl oz |
| | salt and pepper | |
| 75 ml/3 fl oz | couscous | 175 ml/6 fl oz |
| 1 | oranges | 2 |
| 45 ml/3 tbsp | natural yogurt | 90 ml/6 tbsp |
| | dash of extra-virgin olive oil | |
| 1.25 ml/¼ tsp | ground cumin | 2.5 ml/½ tsp |
| 1-2 | spring onions, finely chopped | 2-4 |
| 1 | sticks of celery, finely chopped | 2 |
| | mixed salad leaves, to serve | |
| 25 g/1 oz | vegetarian cheese, grated | 50 g/2 oz |

## One

1. Place the water and a pinch of salt in a medium bowl. Cover and microwave on HIGH for 1-2 minutes, or until the water boils. Stir in the couscous and leave to stand, covered, for 5 minutes to swell the grains.

2. Meanwhile, peel the orange, then cut away the pith and remove the orange segments over a bowl to catch the juices.

3. Beat the yogurt with the orange juices, olive oil, cumin and salt and pepper to taste, blending well.

4. Fluff the couscous with a fork and add the yogurt mixture. Stir in the orange segments, spring onions and celery, mixing well to combine.

5. To serve, line an individual serving plate with the salad leaves, mound the couscous mixture on top and sprinkle with the grated cheese. Serve at once.

## Two

1. Place the water and a pinch of salt in a medium bowl. Cover and microwave on HIGH for 2-3 minutes, or until the water boils. Stir in the couscous and leave to stand, covered, for 5 minutes to swell the grains.

2. Meanwhile, peel the oranges, then cut away the pith and remove the orange segments over a bowl to catch the juices.

3. Beat the yogurt with the orange juices, olive oil, cumin and salt and pepper to taste, blending well.

4. Fluff the couscous with a fork and add the yogurt mixture. Stir in the orange segments, spring onions and celery, mixing well to combine.

5. To serve, line two individual serving plates with the salad leaves, mound the couscous mixture on top and sprinkle with the grated cheese. Serve at once.

# *Sweet and Sour Salad*

The vegetables in this salad are very lightly cooked in the microwave before being tossed in a sweet and sour dressing, then left to cool before serving. Serve as a light lunch dish or special salad accompaniment.

| One | | Two |
|---|---|---|
| 15 ml/1 tbsp | vegetable or groundnut oil | 30 ml/2 tbsp |
| 1 | cloves of garlic, crushed | 2 |
| 4 | spring onions, trimmed and chopped | 8 |
| ½ | yellow pepper, cored, seeded and sliced | 1 |
| ½ | red pepper, cored, seeded and sliced | 1 |
| ½ | green pepper, cored, seeded and sliced | 1 |
| ¼ | bunch of radishes, trimmed and sliced | ½ |
| 175 g/6 oz | Chinese leaves or bok choy, finely shredded | 350 g/12 oz |
| 75 g/3 oz | beansprouts | 175 g/6 oz |
| 15 ml/1 tbsp | wine vinegar | 30 ml/2 tbsp |
| 15 ml/1 tbsp | clear honey | 30 ml/2 tbsp |
| 15 ml/1 tbsp | soy sauce | 30 ml/2 tbsp |
| 2.5 ml/½ tsp | toasted sesame seeds | 5 ml/1 tsp |
| | salt and pepper | |

## One

1. Place the oil in a large bowl and microwave on HIGH for 30 seconds until hot. Add the garlic and spring onions, cover and microwave on HIGH for a further 30 seconds.

2. Add the peppers, mixing well. Cover and microwave on HIGH for 1½-2 minutes, stirring twice.

3. Add the radishes, Chinese leaves or bok choy and beansprouts, mixing well. Cover and microwave on HIGH for 30-60 seconds, or until the vegetables are softened but still have a crispy bite and firm texture. Take care not to overcook at this stage.

4. Meanwhile, mix the vinegar with the honey, soy sauce, sesame seeds and salt and pepper to taste. Stir into the vegetables, tossing well to coat. Transfer to a serving bowl and allow to cool. Toss gently to mix just before serving.

## Two

1. Place the oil in a large bowl and microwave on HIGH for 30 seconds until hot. Add the garlic and spring onions, cover and microwave on HIGH for a further 45-60 seconds.

2. Add the peppers, mixing well. Cover and microwave on HIGH for 2-2½ minutes, stirring twice.

3. Add the radishes, Chinese leaves or bok choy and beansprouts, mixing well. Cover and microwave on HIGH for 45-60 seconds, or until the vegetables are softened but still have a crispy bite and firm texture. Take care not to overcook at this stage.

4. Meanwhile, mix the vinegar with the honey, soy sauce, sesame seeds and salt and pepper to taste. Stir into the vegetables, tossing well to coat. Transfer to a serving bowl and allow to cool. Toss gently to mix just before serving.

# Sweet and Sour Bean and Beetroot Salad

This is a wonderfully flavoursome salad good to serve with an autumnal or winter main meal. It is equally tasty served with bread and cheese to ring the changes to a plain ploughman's lunch.

| One | | Two |
|---|---|---|
| 1 | medium cooked beetroot | 2 |
| 7 g/¼ oz | butter | 15 g/½ oz |
| 5 ml/1 tsp | cider vinegar | 10 ml/2 tsp |
| 5 ml/1 tsp | clear honey | 10 ml/2 tsp |
| 100 g/4 oz | cooked cannellini or haricot beans | 225 g/8 oz |
| 5 ml/1 tsp | snipped chives | 10 ml/2 tsp |
| | salt and pepper | |
| 15 ml/1 tbsp | soured cream or thick plain yogurt | 30 ml/2 tbsp |

## One

1. Peel the beetroot if necessary, then cut into slices. Place in a dish with the butter, cover and microwave on HIGH for 30 seconds, or until the butter melts and coats the beetroot slices.

2. Add the vinegar and honey, mixing well. Cover and microwave on HIGH for a further 30 seconds, stirring once.

3. Add the beans, chives and salt and pepper to taste, mixing well. Spoon into a small serving dish and drizzle over the soured cream or yogurt. Serve warm or cold.

## Two

1. Peel the beetroot if necessary, then cut into slices. Place in a dish with the butter, cover and microwave on HIGH for 45-60 seconds, or until the butter melts and coats the beetroot slices.

2. Add the vinegar and honey, mixing well. Cover and microwave on HIGH for a further 45-60 seconds, stirring once.

3. Add the beans, chives and salt and pepper to taste, mixing well. Spoon into a small serving dish and drizzle over the soured cream or yogurt. Serve warm or cold.

# Hot Three-Beanfeast Salad

If you have some canned beans in the cupboard then you have the makings of a beanfeast of a meal - for this is a marvellous salad made with canned beans and makes a delicious accompaniment to jacket-baked potatoes.

| One | | Two |
|---|---|---|
| 50 g/2 oz | French or thin green beans, topped and tailed | 100 g/4 oz |
| ¼ | small onion, peeled and thinly sliced | ½ |
| ½ | small clove of garlic, crushed | 1 |
| 15 ml/1 tbsp | Italian-style salad dressing | 30 ml/2 tbsp |
| ½ | 200 g/7 oz can borlotti, pinto or red kidney beans, drained and rinsed | 1 |
| ½ | 200 g/7 oz can butter beans, drained and rinsed | 1 |
| 10 ml/2 tsp | snipped chives | 20 ml/4 tsp |
| | salt and pepper | |

## One

1. Place the French or green beans in a medium bowl with the onion, garlic and Italian dressing. Cover and microwave on HIGH for 3 minutes, or until the vegetables are just tender, stirring once.

2. Add the remaining beans, chives and salt and pepper to taste, mixing well. Cover and microwave on HIGH for 1½-2 minutes, or until heated through, stirring once. Serve at once while hot.

## Two

1. Place the French or green beans in a medium bowl with the onion, garlic and Italian dressing. Cover and microwave on HIGH for 4-4½ minutes, or until the vegetables are just tender, stirring once.

2. Add the remaining beans, chives and salt and pepper to taste, mixing well. Cover and microwave on HIGH for 2-3 minutes, or until heated through, stirring once. Serve at once while still hot.

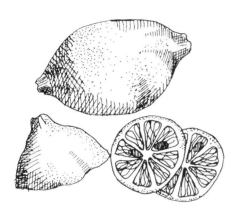

# Parsnips with Crème Fraîche and Rocket

Creamy mashed parsnips are an old favourite – here they have been given a new twist by being mashed with crème fraîche and peppery-tasting chopped rocket.

| One | | Two |
|---|---|---|
| 175 g/6 oz | parsnips, peeled and chopped | 350 g/12 oz |
| 7 g/¼ oz | butter or margarine | 15 g/½ oz |
| 15 ml/1 tbsp | water | 30 ml/2 tbsp |
| 5 ml/1 tsp | lemon juice | 10 ml/2 tsp |
| 25 ml/5 tsp | crème fraîche | 45 ml/3 tbsp |
| 15 ml/1 tbsp | chopped fresh rocket | 30 ml/2 tbsp |
| | salt and pepper | |

## One

1. Place the parsnips in a medium dish with the butter, water and lemon juice. Cover and microwave on HIGH for 3-4 minutes, stirring twice. Leave to stand, covered, for 3 minutes.

2. Drain thoroughly, then mash with the crème fraîche until creamy.

3. Add the chopped rocket and salt and pepper to taste, mixing well. Serve while still hot.

## Two

1. Place the parsnips in a medium dish with the butter, water and lemon juice. Cover and microwave on HIGH for 6-8 minutes, stirring twice. Leave to stand, covered, for 3 minutes.

2. Drain thoroughly, then mash with the crème fraîche until creamy.

3. Add the chopped rocket and salt and pepper to taste, mixing well. Serve while still hot.

# Vegetarian Curried Pilaf

This is a splendid basic curried pilaf dish suitable for serving with other spiced or curried vegetable dishes.

## One                                Two

| One | | Two |
|---|---|---|
| 20 g/¾ oz | butter | 40 g/1½ oz |
| 7.5 ml/1½ tsp | curry powder | 15 ml/1 tbsp |
| ½ | onion, peeled and chopped | 1 |
| 15 ml/1 tbsp | raisins or toasted flaked almonds | 30 ml/2 tbsp |
| 1 | cloves of garlic, crushed | 2 |
| 75 g/3 oz | basmati rice | 175 g/6 oz |
| 175 ml/6 fl oz | half coconut milk and water mixed | 350 ml/12 fl oz |
| 40 g/1½ oz | frozen peas, defrosted | 75 g/3 oz |
| 15 g/½ oz | desiccated coconut | 25 g/1 oz |
| | salt and pepper | |

## One

1. Place the butter in a large bowl and microwave on HIGH for 30-60 seconds, until melted. Stir in the curry powder, onion, raisins or almonds and garlic, mixing well. Microwave on HIGH for 2-3 minutes, stirring once.

2. Add the rice and stir to coat in the curried butter mixture. Microwave on HIGH for 2-3 minutes, stirring once halfway through the cooking time.

3. Add the mixed coconut milk and water and stir well. Cover tightly and microwave on HIGH for 2 minutes. Reduce the power setting to MEDIUM and microwave for 12 minutes, stirring once halfway through the cooking time.

4. Add the peas, coconut and salt and pepper to taste, mixing well. Cover tightly and leave to stand for 5 minutes before serving.

## Two

1. Place the butter in a large bowl and microwave on HIGH for 1-1½ minutes, until melted. Stir in the curry powder, onion, raisins or almonds and garlic, mixing well. Microwave on HIGH for 4 minutes, stirring once.

2. Add the rice and stir to coat in the curried butter mixture. Microwave on HIGH for 4 minutes, stirring once halfway through the cooking time.

3. Add the mixed coconut milk and water and stir well. Cover tightly and microwave on HIGH for 2 minutes. Reduce the power setting to MEDIUM and microwave for 12 minutes, stirring once halfway through the cooking time.

4. Add the peas, coconut and salt and pepper to taste, mixing well. Cover tightly and leave to stand for 5 minutes before serving.

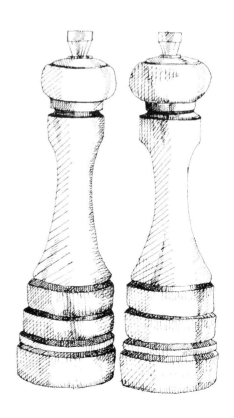

# Thai Fragrant Coconut Rice

This is the finest rice to serve with Thai-style vegetable curries and Thai-inspired dishes. Basmati rice is cooked with creamed coconut, lemon grass, fresh root ginger and spices to make a wonderfully aromatic, fluffy rice.

| One | | Two |
|---|---|---|
| 75 g/3 oz | basmati rice | 175 g/6 oz |
| | small piece of peeled root ginger, sliced | |
| 1 | cloves | 2 |
| | small stem of lemon grass, bruised and halved | |
| 2.5 ml/½ tsp | grated nutmeg | 5 ml/1 tsp |
| | small cinnamon stick | |
| | small bay leaf | |
| | small strip of lime zest | |
| 1.25 ml/¼ tsp | salt | 2.5 ml/½ tsp |
| 7 g/¼ oz | creamed coconut | 15 g/½ oz |
| 150 ml/¼ pt | boiling water | 300 ml/½ pt |

## One and Two

1. Place the rice, ginger, cloves, lemon grass, nutmeg, cinnamon stick, bay leaf, lime zest, salt, creamed coconut and boiling water in a medium bowl and mix well.

2. Cover tightly and microwave on HIGH for 3 minutes. Reduce the power setting to MEDIUM and microwave for a further 12 minutes, stirring twice, or until the rice is tender but still has a bite to it and the liquid has been absorbed.

3. Fluff the rice with a fork to separate the grains. Remove and discard the large pieces of spices before serving.

# Rotini with Roasted Garlic and Courgettes

Rotini are pasta twists or spirals and when combined with roasted garlic and grated courgettes make a wonderful main meal accompaniment or simple light lunch offering.

| One | | Two |
|---|---|---|
| 75 g/3 oz | dried rotini | 175 g/6 oz |
| 600 ml/1 pt | boiling water | 1.2 litres/2 pts |
| 1 | courgettes, grated | 2 |
| ½ | head of Roasted Garlic (see page 85) | 1 |
| 15 ml/1 tbsp | extra-virgin olive oil | 30 ml/2 tbsp |
| 2.5 ml/½ tsp | chopped fresh thyme and rosemary combined | 5 ml/1 tsp |
| | salt and pepper | |

## One and Two

1. Place the pasta in a large bowl and pour over the boiling water. Microwave on HIGH for 10-12 minutes, stirring once halfway through the cooking time, until the pasta is just tender. Add the courgettes, stir well to combine, cover and leave to stand for 3 minutes.

2. Meanwhile, squeeze the roasted garlic from the garlic cloves into a small bowl. Add the oil, herbs and salt and pepper to taste, blending well.

3. Drain the pasta and courgette mixture thoroughly. Add the garlic mixture and toss well to mix. Serve at once.

# Penne with Tomatoes, Red Onion and Courgettes

This is a simple salad-style dish of pasta with seasonal summer or early autumn vegetables. Serve as a light meal or as part of a main meal selection of vegetarian dishes.

| One | | Two |
|---|---|---|
| 75 g/3 oz | dried penne | 175 g/6 oz |
| 600 ml/1 pt | boiling water | 1.2 litres/2 pts |
| 100 g/4 oz | mixed green and yellow courgettes | 225 g/8 oz |
| 1 | tomatoes, skinned, seeded and chopped | 2 |
| ½ | red onion, peeled and thinly sliced | 1 |
| 15 ml/1 tbsp | extra-virgin olive oil | 30 ml/2 tbsp |
| 5 ml/1 tsp | lemon juice | 10 ml/2 tsp |
| 1.25 ml/¼ tsp | grated lemon zest | 2.5 ml/½ tsp |
| 10 ml/2 tsp | chopped fresh parsley | 20 ml/4 tsp |
| | salt and pepper | |

## One and Two

1. Place the pasta in a large bowl and pour over the boiling water. Microwave on HIGH for 10-12 minutes, stirring once halfway through the cooking time, until the pasta is just tender. Allow to stand for 3 minutes, drain well, rinse with cold water to cool quickly, then drain thoroughly.

2. Meanwhile, trim the courgettes and then slice very thinly into rounds. Add to the pasta with the tomato and red onion.

3. Beat the oil with the lemon juice, lemon zest, parsley and salt and pepper to taste. Drizzle over the pasta mixture and toss gently to mix. Serve as soon as possible.

# Peppered Fettucine

This recipe can be made with a single colour pepper or a mixture of colours. Supermarkets now offer a full range including red, yellow, green, orange and black peppers from which to make your selection.

| One | | Two |
|---|---|---|
| 75 g/3 oz | dried fettucine | 175 g/6 oz |
| 600 ml/1 pt | boiling water | 1.2 litres/2 pts |
| 100 g/4 oz | mixed pepper strips | 225 g/8 oz |
| 7.5 ml/1½ tsp | smooth peanut butter | 15 ml/1 tbsp |
| 22.5 ml/1½ tbsp | vegetable stock | 45 ml/3 tbsp |
| | pinch of dried red pepper flakes | |
| 5 ml/1 tsp | soy sauce | 10 ml/2 tsp |
| pinch | ground ginger | 1.25 ml/¼ tsp |
| 3.75 ml/¾ tsp | white wine vinegar | 7.5 ml/1½ tsp |
| | salt and pepper | |

## One

1. Place the pasta in a medium bowl and pour over the boiling water. Microwave on HIGH for 6 minutes, stirring once halfway through the cooking time, until the pasta is just tender. Cover and allow to stand while cooking the pepper mixture.

2. Meanwhile, place the peppers, peanut butter, stock, pepper flakes, soy sauce, ginger, vinegar and salt and pepper to taste in a bowl and microwave on HIGH for 1-2 minutes, stirring twice, or until the sauce is smooth and the peppers are tender crisp.

3. Drain the pasta thoroughly and place in a warmed serving bowl. Add the cooked peppers with their sauce and toss gently to mix. Serve at once.

## Two

1. Place the pasta in a large bowl and pour over the boiling water. Microwave on HIGH for 6 minutes, stirring once halfway through the cooking time, until the pasta is just tender. Allow to stand while cooking the pepper mixture.

2. Meanwhile, place the peppers, peanut butter, stock, pepper flakes, soy sauce, ginger, vinegar and salt and pepper to taste in a bowl and microwave on HIGH for 2-3 minutes, stirring twice, or until the sauce is smooth and the peppers are tender crisp.

3. Drain the pasta thoroughly and place in a warmed serving bowl. Add the cooked peppers with their sauce and toss gently to mix. Serve at once.

# Thai Sesame Hot Noodles

Plain egg noodles taste all the better when tossed in a Thai-inspired mixture made with nutty sesame oil, soy sauce, peanut butter, coriander, lime juice and chilli. Serve hot as a main course accompaniment.

| One | | Two |
|---|---|---|
| 300 ml/½ pt | water | 600 ml/1 pt |
| 75 g/3 oz | medium egg noodles | 175 g/6 oz |
| 7.5 ml/1½ tsp | sunflower oil | 15 ml/1 tbsp |
| 5 ml/1 tsp | sesame oil | 10 ml/2 tsp |
| ½ | small clove of garlic, crushed | 1 |
| 2.5 ml/½ tsp | smooth peanut butter | 5 ml/1 tsp |
| ¼ | small green chilli, seeded and very finely chopped | ½ |
| 7.5 ml/1½ tsp | toasted sesame seeds | 15 ml/1 tbsp |
| 10 ml/2 tsp | light soy sauce | 20 ml/4 tsp |
| 2.5-5 ml/½-1 tsp | lime juice | 5-10 ml/1-2 tsp |
| | salt and pepper | |
| 10 ml/2 tsp | chopped fresh coriander | 20 ml/4 tsp |

## One

1. Place the water in a medium bowl and microwave on HIGH for 3-4 minutes, or until boiling. Add the noodles, stir well, cover and leave to stand for 6 minutes, stirring once halfway through the time. Drain thoroughly.

2. Meanwhile, to make the dressing, mix the oils with the garlic and peanut butter until smooth.

3. Add the chilli, sesame seeds, soy sauce and lime juice, according to taste and mix well. Season to taste with salt and pepper.

4. Add the mixture to the cooked noodles and toss to coat. Microwave on HIGH for 30-45 seconds to reheat. Add the coriander and toss well to mix. Serve at once.

## Two

1. Place the water in a medium bowl and microwave on HIGH for 6-7 minutes, or until boiling. Add the noodles, stir well, cover and leave to stand for 6 minutes, stirring once halfway through the time. Drain thoroughly.

2. Meanwhile, to make the dressing, mix the oils with the garlic and peanut butter until smooth.

3. Add the chilli, sesame seeds, soy sauce and lime juice, according to taste and mix well. Season to taste with salt and pepper.

4. Add the mixture to the cooked noodles and toss to coat. Microwave on HIGH for 30-60 seconds to reheat. Add the coriander and toss well to mix. Serve at once.

# Curried Raisin and Mint Couscous

This is a delicious accompaniment to a vegetable curry instead of the usual rice. Serve warm.

| One | | Two |
|---|---|---|
| 5 ml/1 tsp | olive oil | 10 ml/2 tsp |
| ½ | onion, peeled and finely chopped | 1 |
| ½ | clove of garlic, crushed | 1 |
| 1.25 ml/¼ tsp | curry powder | 2.5 ml/½ tsp |
| 125 ml/4 fl oz | vegetable stock | 250 ml/8 fl oz |
| 22.5 ml/1½ tbsp | raisins | 45 ml/3 tbsp |
| 75 ml/3 fl oz | instant couscous | 175 ml/6 fl oz |
| 22.5 ml/1½ tbsp | chopped fresh mint | 45 ml/3 tbsp |
| | salt and pepper | |

## One

1. Place the oil in a medium bowl with the onion and garlic. Cover and microwave on HIGH for 1 minute, stirring once.

2. Add the curry powder, mixing well. Cover and microwave on HIGH for a further 1 minute.

3. Place the vegetable stock in a medium bowl, cover and microwave on HIGH for 1-2 minutes until boiling. Stir in the raisins and couscous and leave to stand, covered, for 5 minutes to allow the grains to swell.

4. Fluff the couscous grains with a fork, add the curried onion mixture with the mint and salt and pepper to taste and mix gently. Serve as soon as possible.

## Two

1. Place the oil in a medium bowl with the onion and garlic. Cover and microwave on HIGH for 1½ minutes, stirring once.

2. Add the curry powder, mixing well. Cover and microwave on HIGH for a further 1½ minutes.

3. Place the vegetable stock in a medium bowl, cover and microwave on HIGH for 1½ - 2½ minutes until boiling. Stir in the raisins and couscous and leave to stand, covered, for 5 minutes to allow the grains to swell.

4. Fluff the couscous grains with a fork, add the curried onion mixture with the mint and salt and pepper to taste and mix gently. Serve as soon as possible.

# New Wave Garlic Bread

New wave-style garlic bread boasts lashings of garlic butter, herbs and grated vegetarian Parmesan cheese. Serve it with barbecue fare or Italian-style dishes.

| One | | Two |
|---|---|---|
| 1 | long, finger-shaped, crusty bread rolls or individual French sticks | 2 |
| 25 g/1 oz | butter | 50 g/2 oz |
| 1 | cloves of garlic, crushed | 2 |
| | small pinch of ground Szechuan pepper | |
| | dash of Chinese chilli sauce | |
| 10 ml/2 tsp | snipped fresh chives | 20 ml/4 tsp |
| 10 ml/2 tsp | chopped fresh coriander | 20 ml/4 tsp |
| 15 ml/1 tbsp | grated vegetarian Parmesan cheese | 30 ml/2 tbsp |

## One

1. Cut the bread roll in half horizontally or make diagonal slits, almost to the base of the roll but not quite through, at regular intervals.

2. Beat the butter with the garlic, pepper, chilli sauce, chives, coriander and Parmesan cheese until well blended. Spread on both sides of the bread roll and sandwich together again or spread between the slits.

3. Loosely wrap in absorbent kitchen paper and microwave on HIGH for 30 to 60 seconds, until the bread is warm and the butter has just melted. Serve at once whilst the bread is still warm.

## Two

1. Cut the bread rolls in half horizontally or make diagonal slits, almost to the base of the rolls but not quite through, at regular intervals.

2. Beat the butter with the garlic, pepper, chilli sauce, chives, coriander and Parmesan cheese until well blended. Spread on both sides of the bread rolls and sandwich together again or spread between the slits.

3. Loosely wrap in absorbent kitchen paper and microwave on HIGH for 1-1½ minutes, until the bread is warm and the butter has just melted. Serve at once whilst the bread is still warm.

# Poppadoms

Plain or spiced there is nothing quite like a crispy poppadom with a flavoursome curry. The bonus of cooking them in the microwave is that no additional oil is required so the poppadom remains a low-fat accompaniment.

| One | | Two |
|---|---|---|
| 1 | plain or spiced poppadoms | 2 |

## One

1. Place the poppadom on the base of the microwave or on the turntable and microwave on HIGH for 20-25 seconds, or until puffy and bubbling.

2. Remove with a spatula to a wire rack and leave for about 15 seconds to crisp.

## Two

1. Place the poppadoms on the base of the microwave or on the turntable so that they do not touch or overlap. Microwave on HIGH for 45-60 seconds, or until puffy and bubbling.

2. Remove with a spatula to a wire rack and leave for about 15 seconds to crisp.

# Flowerpot or Jug Bread

A handy packet of bread mix is all you need to make two flowerpot or measuring-jug shaped loaves of bread. These are perfect for slicing into rounds for serving with soups, cheese as a ploughman's and as a simple bread and butter accompaniment. The bread does stale quickly so is best eaten on the day of making but will keep overnight if wrapped tightly in cling film.

### To make two x 600ml/1 pt loaves

| |
|---|
| 1  280 g/10 oz  packet white or brown bread mix |
| 300 ml/½ pt  hand-hot water |
| oil, for greasing |
| 45-60 ml/3-4 tbsp  toasted sesame seeds, toasted chopped nuts or toasted sunflower seeds or mixture, to coat |

1. Place the bread mix in a bowl and gradually beat in the water to make a smooth, thickened batter. Continue to beat for a further 10 minutes or until the dough is very smooth and elastic.

2. Oil the sides and base of two 600 ml/1 pt glass measuring jugs or very well scrubbed and oiled clay flowerpots. Coat the base and sides with the seeds and/or nuts. Divide the dough between each, cover loosely with cling film and leave in a warm place to rise until doubled in size.

3. Remove the film and microwave on HIGH for 3½-4 minutes, until the dough is cooked and firm. Leave to stand in the jugs or pots for 2 minutes before turning out on to a wire rack to cool.

4. Serve warm or cold, cut into thick or thin rounds to suit.

# SWEET ENDINGS

## *Italian Baked Nectarine*

Plump and juicy, nectarines seem the perfect fruit to eat plain. But when stuffed with an almond macaroon mixture and drizzled with port they are unforgettable. Try the same recipe with yellow, golden or white-fleshed peaches if you prefer.

| One | | Two |
|---|---|---|
| 20 g/¾ oz | almond macaroons | 40 g/1½ oz |
| 7 g/¼ oz | butter | 15 g/½ oz |
| 10 ml/2 tsp | toasted flaked almonds | 20 ml/4 tsp |
| 5 ml/1 tsp | clear honey | 10 ml/2 tsp |
| 1 | large, ripe nectarines | 2 |
| 15 ml/1 tbsp | port | 30 ml/2 tbsp |

## One

1. Crush the macaroons to make coarse crumbs and place in a bowl with the butter, half the flaked almonds and honey. Mix well to blend lightly.

2. Halve the nectarine and remove the stone. Fill the cavities left by the stone with the stuffing mixture and arrange in a shallow cooking dish.

3. Drizzle over the port and cover loosely with cling film. Microwave on HIGH for 1-1½ minutes or until the nectarine is just soft.

4. Decorate with the remaining toasted almonds and spoon over the cooking juices to serve.

## Two

1. Crush the macaroons to make coarse crumbs and place in a bowl with the butter, half the flaked almonds and honey. Mix well to blend lightly.

2. Halve the nectarines and remove the stones. Fill the cavities left by the stone with the stuffing mixture and arrange in a shallow cooking dish.

3. Drizzle over the port and cover loosely with cling film. Microwave on HIGH for 1½-2 minutes or until the nectarines are just soft.

4. Decorate with the remaining toasted almonds and spoon over the cooking juices to serve.

# Nursery Rice Pudding with Dried Apricots

A time-honoured and classic nursery favourite, Rice Pudding is hard to beat as a soothing and satisfying dessert. This recipe with apricots introduces a fruity undertone to the creamy rice and is delicious served hot or cold.

| One | | Two |
|---|---|---|
| 45 ml/3 tbsp | round-grain or pudding rice (level measures) | 90 ml/6 tbsp |
| 15 ml/1 tbsp | sugar | 30 ml/2 tbsp |
| 300 ml/½ pt | milk | 600 ml/1 pt |
| | small knob of butter | |
| | pinch of freshly grated nutmeg | |
| 25 g/1 oz | no-need-to-soak dried apricots, snipped into small pieces | 50 g/2 oz |

## One

1. Place the rice, sugar, milk, butter and nutmeg to taste in a medium bowl and mix well.

2. Microwave on HIGH for 5 minutes, or until the milk boils, stirring once halfway through the cooking time.

3. Reduce the power level to LOW and microwave for 10 minutes, stirring twice.

4. Add the apricots, cover and microwave on LOW for a further 7-10 minutes, or until the rice is soft and the mixture is creamy. Leave to stand for 2 minutes before serving hot, or allow to cool, then chill before serving cold.

## Two

1. Place the rice, sugar, milk, butter and nutmeg to taste in a large bowl and mix well.

2. Microwave on HIGH for 8 minutes, or until the milk boils, stirring once halfway through the cooking time.

3. Reduce the power level to LOW and microwave for 15 minutes, stirring twice.

4. Add the apricots, cover and microwave on LOW for a further 15-20 minutes, or until the rice is soft and the mixture is creamy. Leave to stand for 2 minutes before serving hot, or allow to cool, then chill before serving cold.

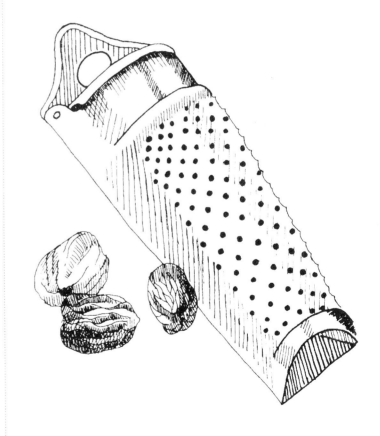

# Creole Bananas

When an instant dessert is required reach no further than the fruit bowl. Peel and halve a banana, dot with butter and sprinkle with white rum and sugar and microwave until softened. Serve topped with lashings of cream and a sprinkling of chopped nuts to conjure up memories of warm tropical nights in faraway places.

| One | | Two |
|---|---|---|
| 1 | large bananas | 2 |
| 2.5 ml/½ tsp | butter, softened | 5 ml/1 tsp |
| 7.5 ml/1½ tsp | lemon juice | 15 ml/1 tbsp |
| 7.5 ml/1½ tsp | caster sugar | 15 ml/1 tbsp |
| 7.5 ml/1½ tsp | white rum | 15 ml/1 tbsp |
| | whipped cream and chopped nuts, to decorate (*optional*) | |

## One

1. Peel and halve the banana lengthwise. Place in a shallow cooking or serving dish.

2. Dot with the butter, then sprinkle with the lemon juice, sugar and white rum.

3. Microwave on HIGH for 2-2½ minutes, rearranging once halfway through the cooking time.

4. Allow to stand for 1 minute before serving topped with whipped cream and chopped nuts, if you like.

## Two

1. Peel and halve the bananas lengthwise. Place in a shallow cooking dish or two small serving dishes.

2. Dot with the butter, then sprinkle with the lemon juice, sugar and white rum.

3. Microwave on HIGH for 3-4 minutes, rearranging twice during the cooking time.

4. Allow to stand for 1 minute before serving topped with whipped cream and chopped nuts, if you like.

# Apple and Cinnamon Crumble with Honey-Sweetened Fromage Frais

I first tried this recipe at Champney's health resort. It's a sort of spiced apple purée topped with a crunchy oaty crumble. For best presentation cook in plastic scone cutters rather than small dishes and remove at the very last minute.

| One | | Two |
|---|---|---|
| 100 g/4 oz | peeled, cored and sliced dessert apples | 225 g/8 oz |
| pinch | ground cinnamon | 1.25 ml/¼ tsp |
| | dash of orange or lemon juice | |
| 25 g/1 oz | butter or margarine | 50 g/2 oz |
| 25 g/1 oz | plain wholemeal flour | 50 g/2 oz |
| 15 g/½ oz | rolled oats | 25 g/1 oz |
| 15 g/½ oz | soft brown sugar | 25 g/1 oz |
| 45 ml/3 tbsp | natural fromage frais | 90 ml/6 tbsp |
| 7.5 ml/1½ tsp | honey | 15 ml/1 tbsp |

## One

1. Place the apples in a small dish with the cinnamon and lemon or orange juice, mixing well.

2. Place a large plastic scone or biscuit cutter in the middle of a cooking and serving plate and spoon the apple mixture into the centre. Alternatively spoon into a small heatproof dish.

3. Rub the butter into the flour until the mixture resembles fine breadcrumbs. Stir in the oats and sugar, mixing well. Spoon on top of the fruit in the cutter pressing down lightly. Microwave on HIGH for 4-5 minutes until cooked.

4. Meanwhile, mix the fromage frais with the honey, blending well.

5. Carefully remove the plastic cutter from around the cooked crumble and, if you like, brown the crumble under a preheated hot grill until golden. Serve warm with the honey-sweetened fromage frais.

## Two

1. Place the apples in a small dish with the cinnamon and lemon or orange juice, mixing well.

2. Place two large plastic cutters into the middle of two individual cooking and serving plates and spoon the apple mixture evenly into the centre. Alternatively spoon into two small heatproof dishes.

3. Rub the butter into the flour until the mixture resembles fine breadcrumbs. Stir in the oats and sugar, mixing well. Spoon on top of the fruit in the cutters, pressing down lightly. Microwave both plates on HIGH for 8-10 minutes until cooked. Alternatively cook the plates separately for 4-5 minutes each.

4. Meanwhile, mix the fromage frais with the honey, blending well.

5. Carefully remove the plastic cutters from around the cooked crumbles and, if you like, brown the crumbles under a preheated hot grill until golden. Serve warm with the honey-sweetened fromage frais.

# Honey and Marzipan Baked Apples

Few puddings are better in the autumn than baked apples stuffed with a dried fruit, honey and marzipan mixture. Serve with a scoop of real dairy ice cream for a decadent dessert.

| One | | Two |
|---|---|---|
| 1 | large cooking or tart dessert apples, cored | 2 |
| 15 ml/1 tbsp | dried fruit (raisins, dates, sultanas, currants or apricots, for example) | 30 ml/2 tbsp |
| 15 ml/1 tbsp | clear honey | 30 ml/2 tbsp |
| 7 g/¼ oz | marzipan or almond paste | 15 g/½ oz |
| 30 ml/2 tbsp | cider or apple juice | 60 ml/4 tbsp |

## One

1. Make a shallow cut around the middle of the apple to prevent it from bursting during cooking. Stand in a shallow cooking dish.

2. Mix the dried fruit with half of the honey and use to stuff the centre of the apple. Top with the piece of marzipan or almond paste. Drizzle with the remaining honey. Pour the cider or apple juice around the apple.

3. Microwave on HIGH for 3-3½ minutes until tender, turning the dish once. Leave to stand for 2 minutes before serving with ice cream, if you like.

## Two

1. Make a shallow cut around the middle of each apple to prevent them from bursting during cooking. Stand in a shallow cooking dish.

2. Mix the dried fruit with half of the honey and use to stuff the centre of the apples. Top each with an equal quantity of marzipan or almond paste. Drizzle with the remaining honey. Pour the cider or apple juice around the apples.

3. Microwave on HIGH for 5-6 minutes until tender, turning the dish once. Leave to stand for 2 minutes before serving with ice cream, if you like.

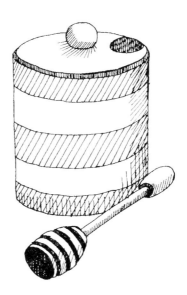

# Fig and Macaroon Trifles

This wonderfully decadent dessert is made in a trice, especially if you use ready-made custard. Prepare in a glass dish so that the rich dark hues of the figs can be seen nestling against the creamy custard layer.

| One | | Two |
|---|---|---|
| 40 g/1½ oz | small macaroons | 75 g/3 oz |
| 30 ml/2 tbsp | Amaretto liqueur | 60 ml/4 tbsp |
| 25 g/1 oz | apricot jam | 50 g/2 oz |
| 75 g/3 oz | fresh figs | 175 g/6 oz |
| 120 ml/8 tbsp | ready-made custard | 250 ml/8 fl oz |
| 75 ml/5 tbsp | double cream | 150 ml/¼ pt |

## One

1. Place the macaroons in the base of an individual glass serving dish.

2. Put the Amaretto liqueur and apricot jam in a small jug and microwave on HIGH for 30-45 seconds, or until the mixture is hot and syrupy, stirring once. Spoon over the macaroons.

3. Slice the figs and layer over the macaroons. Top with the ready-made custard.

4. Whip the cream until it stands in soft peaks, then swirl or pipe over the top of the custard. Chill well before serving.

## Two

1. Divide the macaroons in half and place in the base of two individual glass serving dishes.

2. Put the Amaretto liqueur and apricot jam in a small jug and microwave on HIGH for 1-1¼ minutes, or until the mixture is hot and syrupy, stirring once. Spoon over the macaroons.

3. Slice the figs and layer over the macaroons. Top with the ready-made custard.

4. Whip the cream until it stands in soft peaks, then swirl or pipe over the top of the custard. Chill well before serving.

# Honeyed Grappa Figs

Serve this heavenly dessert of figs moistened with grappa and drizzled with honey with a scoop of clotted cream.

| One | | Two |
|---|---|---|
| 3 | large, plump, purple figs, peeled and halved | 6 |
| | splash of Grappa or brandy | |
| 15 ml/1 tbsp | orange blossom or heather honey | 30 ml/2 tbsp |
| | clotted cream, to serve | |
| | mint sprigs, to decorate | |

## One

1. Place the figs in an individual shallow serving dish, cut sides up. Moisten with a little Grappa or brandy to taste and drizzle over the honey.

2. Microwave on HIGH for 45-60 seconds, until hot and bubbly.

3. Add a scoop of clotted cream, decorate with a mint sprig and serve at once.

## Two

1. Place the figs in two shallow individual serving dishes, cut sides up. Moisten with a little Grappa or brandy to taste and drizzle evenly with the honey.

2. Microwave on HIGH for 1½-2 minutes, until hot and bubbly.

3. Add a scoop of clotted cream to each, decorate each with a mint sprig and serve at once.

*Italian Baked Nectarines (page 112)*

# Boozy Woozy Sponges with Orange Custard Sauce

As you can see from this recipe title here we have a recipe for some light orange sponges served with an intoxicating orange custard sauce. They are so light and scrumptious my husband tells me that grown men can easily eat two of these sponges!

| One | | Two |
|---|---|---|
| 1 small | orange | 1 medium |
| 2-3 | sugar cubes | 5 |
| 40 g/1½ oz | self-raising flour | 75 g/3 oz |
| 25 g/1 oz | soft margarine | 50 g/2 oz |
| 20 g/¾ oz | caster sugar | 40 g/1½ oz |
| ½ | egg | 1 |
| 15 ml/1 tbsp | orange liqueur | 30 ml/2 tbsp |
| | **Custard Sauce:** | |
| 5 ml/1 tsp | cornflour | 10 ml/2 tsp |
| 125 ml/4 fl oz | milk | 250 ml/8 fl oz |
| ½ | egg | 1 |
| 7.5 ml/1½ tsp | caster sugar | 15 ml/1 tbsp |
| 7.5 ml/1½ tsp | orange liqueur | 15 ml/1 tbsp |

## One

1. Microwave the orange on HIGH for 45 seconds. Rub the sugar cubes over the surface to extract as much zest as possible. Crush the cubes and mix with the flour, margarine, sugar and egg, beating well to make a smooth mixture. Cut a thick round slice from the orange and cut away the peel and pith. Place in the bottom of a buttered 250 ml/8 fl oz small pudding bowl.

2. Cover with the prepared sponge mixture and microwave on HIGH for 1-1½ minutes, until just set. Allow to stand for 3 minutes; then turn out on to a small serving dish and sprinkle with the orange liqueur. Keep warm while preparing the custard sauce.

3. To make the custard sauce, mix the cornflour with 15 ml/1 tbsp of the milk. Beat in the egg. Place the remaining milk in a jug with the sugar and microwave on HIGH for about 1¼-1½ minutes until hot. Whisk into the egg mixture, then microwave on HIGH for a further 1 minute, whisking twice to keep the sauce smooth and thickened. Add the liqueur, mixing well.

4. Pour the custard around the base of the warm sponge and serve at once.

## Two

1. Microwave the orange on HIGH for 1 minute. Rub the sugar cubes over the surface to extract as much zest as possible. Crush the sugar cubes and mix with the flour, margarine, sugar and egg, beating well to make a smooth mixture. Cut two thick round slices from the orange and cut away the peel and pith. Place in the bottom of two buttered 250 ml/8 fl oz pudding bowls.

2. Cover with the prepared sponge mixture and microwave on HIGH for 2-2½ minutes, or until just set. Allow to stand for 3 minutes, then turn each out on to a warmed serving plate and sprinkle evenly with the orange liqueur. Keep warm while preparing the sauce.

3. To make the custard sauce, mix the cornflour with 30 ml/2 tbsp of the milk. Beat in the egg. Place the remaining milk in a jug with the sugar and microwave on HIGH for 2 minutes until hot. Whisk into the egg mixture, then microwave on HIGH for a further 1½ minutes, whisking twice to keep the sauce smooth and thickened. Add the liqueur, mixing well.

4. Pour the custard around the bases of the warm sponges and serve at once.

*Boozy Woozy Sponges with Orange Custard Sauce, back (page 117) and Sozzled Summer Pudding, front (page 122)*

# Pears in Gingered Cider

The fruity mellowness of cider when combined with fragrant pear juices is stunning as you will see with this warm pear dessert. Serve with crisp dessert biscuits and crème fraîche.

| One | | Two |
|---|---|---|
| 25 g/1 oz | caster sugar | 50 g/2 oz |
| 150 ml/¼ pt | dry cider | 300 ml/½ pt |
| 2 | thin slices of fresh root ginger | 4 |
| 1 | large, ripe but firm pears | 2 |
| 2.5 ml/½ tsp | arrowroot powder (or cornflour if unavailable) | 5 ml/1 tsp |
| | crisp dessert biscuits and crème fraîche, to serve | |

## One

1. Place the sugar, cider and root ginger in a medium bowl and microwave on HIGH for 4 minutes, stirring twice to dissolve the sugar and to bring the syrup to a good boil.

2. Meanwhile, peel and halve the pear, leaving the stalk intact on one half and add to the hot syrup. Cover loosely and microwave on HIGH for 2-3 minutes, until tender, rearranging the pears once and spooning the syrup over the pears halfway through the cooking time.

3. Remove the pears from the syrup with a slotted spoon and place on a warmed serving plate.

4. Remove and discard the ginger slices from the syrup. Blend the arrowroot or cornflour with a little cold water, then stir into the syrup, blending well. Microwave on HIGH for 1 minute, stirring twice, to ensure the syrup thickens smoothly and evenly.

5. Pour the thickened sauce over the pears and serve warm with crisp dessert biscuits and crème fraîche.

## Two

1. Place the sugar, cider and root ginger in a large bowl and microwave on HIGH for 5 minutes, stirring twice to dissolve the sugar and to bring the syrup to a good boil.

2. Meanwhile, peel and halve the pears, leaving the stalks intact on two of the halves and add to the hot syrup. Cover loosely and microwave on HIGH for 3-5 minutes, until tender, rearranging the pears once and spooning the syrup over the pears halfway through the cooking time.

3. Remove the pears from the syrup with a slotted spoon and place on two warmed individual serving plates.

4. Remove and discard the ginger slices from the syrup. Blend the arrowroot or cornflour with a little cold water, then stir into the syrup, blending well. Microwave on HIGH for 1½ minutes, stirring twice, to ensure the syrup thickens smoothly and evenly.

5. Pour the thickened sauce over the pears and serve warm with crisp dessert biscuits and crème fraîche.

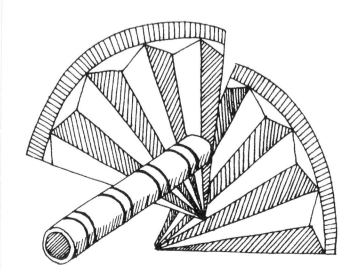

# Poached Fruit in Champagne

If I am to believe a popular newspaper, then the staple in many single male's refrigerator is a bottle of champagne. I presume it is mainly for liquid consumption rather than for cooking but imagining that there might be a few dregs leftover, I have concocted this fruit dish using just a dash or two. It makes a good dessert dish but also a wonderful light breakfast for one or two. Needless to say any other wine may be substituted or even cider.

| One | | Two |
|---|---|---|
| 5 ml/1 tsp | sugar | 10 ml/2 tsp |
| 30 ml/2 tbsp | champagne | 60 ml/4 tbsp |
| 5 ml/1 tsp | lemon juice | 10 ml/2 tsp |
| 175 g/6 oz | mixed prepared fruit (pear, nectarine, apple, plum or berries, for example) | 350 g/12 oz |

## One

1. Place the sugar and the champagne in a medium bowl and microwave on HIGH for 2 minutes.

2. Add the lemon juice and stir well to ensure that all the sugar has dissolved to make a light syrup.

3. Add the prepared fruit, cut into bite-sized pieces and mix well. Loosely cover and microwave on HIGH for 3-5 minutes until the fruit is tender, stirring twice. The timing will very much depend upon the fruit used - a mixture with predominantly hard fruits like apples and pears taking longer than a light fruit mixture of berries and other soft fruits.

4. Leave to stand for 2-3 minutes before serving with yogurt if you like.

## Two

1. Place the sugar and the champagne in a large bowl and microwave on HIGH for 3 minutes.

2. Add the lemon juice and stir well to ensure that all the sugar has dissolved to make a light syrup.

3. Add the prepared fruit, cut into bite-sized pieces and mix well. Loosely cover and microwave on HIGH for 4-6 minutes until the fruit is tender, stirring twice. The timing will very much depend upon the fruit used - a mixture with predominantly hard fruits like apples and pears taking longer than a light fruit mixture of berries and other soft fruits.

4. Leave to stand for 2-3 minutes before serving with yogurt if you like.

# Grand Marnier and Rhubarb Fool

This is the English classic dessert with a hint of French sophistication. If you prefer, the low-fat vanilla yogurt can be replaced with softly whipped cream.

| One | | Two |
|---|---|---|
| 100 g/4 oz | rhubarb, trimmed and sliced | 225 g/8 oz |
| 25 g/1 oz | sugar | 50 g/2 oz |
| 7.5 ml/1½ tsp | orange juice | 15 ml/1 tbsp |
| 7.5 ml/1½ tsp | Grand Marnier | 15 ml/1 tbsp |
| 125 ml/4 fl oz | low-fat vanilla yogurt | 250 ml/8 fl oz |

## One

1. Place the rhubarb, sugar and orange juice in a bowl, mixing well. Cover loosely and microwave on HIGH for 3-3½ minutes, stirring once halfway through the cooking time until tender. Leave to stand, covered, for 3 minutes.

2. Stir the Grand Marnier into the rhubarb, beating well, cool, then chill until ready for serving.

3. To serve, alternate layers of the rhubarb mixture and the vanilla yogurt in a large wine goblet or dessert dish. Using a small knife or skewer, swirl the mixtures together to give a marbled effect. Serve as soon as possible.

## Two

1. Place the rhubarb, sugar and orange juice in a bowl, mixing well. Cover loosely and microwave on HIGH for 5-6 minutes, stirring once halfway through the cooking time until tender. Leave to stand, covered, for 3 minutes.

2. Stir the Grand Marnier into the rhubarb, beating well, cool, then chill until ready for serving.

3. To serve, alternate layers of the rhubarb mixture and the vanilla yogurt in two large wine goblets or dessert dishes. Using a small knife or skewer, swirl the mixtures together to give a marbled effect. Serve as soon as possible.

# Pink Grapefruit with Cassis

This has to be one of the prettiest, easiest and most economical desserts I know. Serve well chilled with crisp dessert biscuits.

| One | | Two |
|---|---|---|
| 1 | large pink grapefruits | 2 |
| 15 ml/1 tbsp | sugar | 30 ml/2 tbsp |
| 11.25 ml/2¼ tsp | water | 22.5 ml/1½ tbsp |
| 15 ml/1 tbsp | crème de cassis | 30 ml/2 tbsp |
| | mint sprigs and fresh blackcurrants to decorate (*optional*) | |
| | crisp dessert biscuits, to serve | |

## One

1. Peel the grapefruit, removing the skin and any white pith over a bowl to catch any juices. Cut between the membranes to release the segments of grapefruit. Squeeze any excess juice from the membrane into the bowl.

2. Place the grapefruit juice, sugar and water in a small bowl and microwave on HIGH for about 1-2 minutes, stirring twice until the sugar dissolves and the mixture becomes syrupy.

3. Carefully add the cassis (taking care since the sugar mixture is very hot and may spit and bubble), mixing well.

4. Arrange the grapefruit segments on a serving plate and drizzle over the cassis syrup. Chill thoroughly before serving decorated with mint sprigs and fresh blackcurrants accompanied with crisp dessert biscuits.

## Two

1. Peel the grapefruit, removing the skin and any white pith over a bowl to catch any juices. Cut between the membranes to release the segments of grapefruit. Squeeze any excess juice from the membrane into the bowl.

2. Place the grapefruit juice, sugar and water in a small bowl and microwave on HIGH for about 1½-2½ minutes, stirring twice until the sugar dissolves and the mixture becomes syrupy.

3. Carefully add the cassis (taking care since the sugar mixture is very hot and may spit and bubble), mixing well.

4. Arrange the grapefruit segments equally on two serving plates and drizzle over the cassis syrup. Chill thoroughly before serving decorated with mint sprigs and fresh blackcurrants, accompanied with crisp dessert biscuits.

# Chocolate Cups with Brandied Cream Billows

Chocolate cups are perfect for serving scoops of brandied syllabub, drizzled with caramel. When time is short use ready-made shells found in many supermarkets.

| One | | Two |
|---|---|---|
| 25 g/1 oz | plain chocolate | 50 g/2 oz |
| | OR | |
| 1 | ready-made chocolate shells | 2 |
| 15 g/½ oz | sugar | 25 g/1 oz |
| 7.5 ml/1½ tsp | water | 15 ml/1 tbsp |
| 5 ml/1 tsp | brandy | 10 ml/2 tsp |
| 45 ml/3 tbsp | double cream | 90 ml/6 tbsp |

## One

1. Break the chocolate into pieces in a bowl and microwave on MEDIUM for 1½-1¾ minutes, stirring twice until smooth.

2. Spoon the chocolate into a double-thickness paper bun baking case and spread over the base and sides with the back of a spoon to form a chocolate cup. Carefully turn upside down on to a greaseproof-paper-lined plate and chill until set.

3. Meanwhile, place the sugar and water in a small heatproof bowl and microwave on HIGH for 1-1½ minutes until golden brown. Carefully add the brandy (taking care as the mixture will splutter) and mix well.

4. Place the cream in a small bowl with half of the brandied caramel mixture and whip until soft peaks form.

5. Carefully peel the paper case away from the chocolate cup and place on a serving plate. Spoon the brandied caramel syllabub into the chocolate cup so that it billows like soft clouds. Drizzle with the remaining caramel and serve at once.

## Two

1. Break the chocolate into pieces in a bowl and microwave on MEDIUM for 2-2½ minutes, stirring twice until smooth.

2. Spoon the chocolate evenly into two double-thickness paper bun baking cases and spread over the bases and sides with the back of a spoon to form two chocolate cups. Carefully turn each upside down on to a greaseproof-paper-lined plate and chill until set.

3. Meanwhile, place the sugar and water in a small heatproof bowl and microwave on HIGH for 2-2½ minutes until golden brown. Carefully add the brandy (taking care as the mixture will splutter) and mix well.

4. Place the cream in a small bowl with half of the brandied caramel mixture and whip until soft peaks form.

5. Carefully peel the paper cases away from the chocolate cups and place on two individual serving plates. Spoon the brandied caramel syllabub into the chocolate cups so that they billow like soft clouds. Drizzle with the remaining caramel and serve at once.

# Sozzled Summer Pudding

I don't know a soul who hasn't drooled over this summer pudding recipe where the fruits are cooked in a little reviving spirit. I have experimented with brandy, crème de cassis, white wine and even pear brandy for cooking the fruit and each and every one was an unmitigated success. Select the tipple you like best or finish the dregs in the drinks cupboard and if you find it bare ... then use fruit juice or water.

| One | | Two |
|---|---|---|
| 3 | slices of day-old white bread or thinly sliced sweet brioche | 6 |
| 150 g/5 oz | assorted fresh berry fruits (strawberries, raspberries, loganberries, blackberries or fresh stoned cherries, for example) | 300 g/10 oz |
| 22.5 ml/1½ tbsp | caster sugar | 45 ml/3 tbsp |
| 22.5 ml/1½ tbsp | brandy, crème de cassis, sherry, cider, fruit juice or water | 45 ml/3 tbsp |
| | soured cream, to serve | |

## One

1. Trim the crusts from the bread slices and cut into fingers. Use about three-quarters of the fingers to line the base and sides of a small (150 ml/¼ pt) ramekin dish or teacup. The bread slices must fit snugly together so that no gaps remain.

2. Place the fruit in a small bowl with the sugar and chosen liquor. Cover loosely and microwave on HIGH for 4-5 minutes, stirring twice, until the fruit is softened and juices have formed.

3. Remove the fruit from the dish with a slotted spoon and spoon into the bread-lined dish, reserving the juices.

4. Cover the fruit mixture with the remaining bread fingers. Place a small saucer on top with a weight to press down on the pudding and chill overnight.

5. To serve, invert the pudding on to an individual serving plate and spoon over the reserved fruit cooking juices. Serve with a dollop of soured cream.

## Two

1. Trim the crusts from the bread slices and cut into fingers. Use about three-quarters of the fingers to line the base and sides of two small (150 ml/¼ pt) ramekin dishes or teacups. The bread slices must fit snugly together so that no gaps remain.

2. Place the fruit in a medium bowl with the sugar and chosen liquor. Cover loosely and microwave on HIGH for 6-7 minutes, stirring twice, until the fruit is softened and juices have formed.

3. Remove the fruit from the dish with a slotted spoon and spoon into the bread-lined dishes, reserving the juices.

4. Cover the fruit mixture with the remaining bread fingers. Place a small saucer on top of each one with a weight to press down on the puddings and chill overnight.

5. To serve, invert the puddings on to two individual serving plates and spoon over the reserved fruit cooking juices. Serve each with a dollop of soured cream.

# Summer Fruit Cups

Fresh summer berry fruits need just the minimum of cooking to make a super sauce for coating more of the same. Chill thoroughly before serving with yogurt, crème fraîche or soured cream.

| One | | Two |
|---|---|---|
| 25 g/1 oz | redcurrants, topped and tailed | 50 g/2 oz |
| 50 g/2 oz | raspberries, hulled | 100 g/4 oz |
| 15 g/½ oz | caster sugar | 25 g/1 oz |
| 5 ml/1 tsp | water or fruit juice | 10 ml/2 tsp |
| 7.5 ml/1½ tsp | Kirsch | 15 ml/1 tbsp |
| 100 g/4 oz | mixed prepared summer berry fruits (raspberries, strawberries, blueberries and loganberries, for example) | 225 g/8 oz |
| | mint sprigs, to decorate | |

## One

1. Place the redcurrants, raspberries and sugar in a small bowl with the water or fruit juice. Cover tightly and microwave on HIGH for 2-3 minutes, stirring twice until the berries are tender and juicy. Transfer to a food processor or blender and purée until smooth, then sieve to remove any pips. Alternatively, press through a fine nylon sieve. Allow to cool, then stir in the Kirsch.

2. Spoon the prepared fruit berries into an individual serving dish and spoon over the prepared fruit sauce to serve.

3. Decorate with mint sprigs and serve with a drizzle or dollop of yogurt, crème fraîche or soured cream.

## Two

1. Place the redcurrants, raspberries and sugar in a medium bowl with the water or fruit juice. Cover tightly and microwave on HIGH for 3-3½ minutes, stirring twice until the berries are tender and juicy. Transfer to a food processor or blender and purée until smooth, then sieve to remove any pips. Alternatively, press through a fine nylon sieve. Allow to cool, then stir in the Kirsch.

2. Divide the prepared fruit berries between two individual serving dishes and spoon over the prepared fruit sauce to serve.

3. Decorate with mint sprigs and serve with a drizzle or dollop of yogurt, crème fraîche or soured cream.

# *Heaven-Sent Chocolate Creams*

Here is an utterly irresistible chocolate creation to round-off a meal. Decorate with chocolate caraque, chocolate leaves or chocolate curls for an impressive look.

| One | | Two |
|---|---|---|
| 50 g/2 oz | plain chocolate | 100 g/4 oz |
| 10 ml/2 tsp | golden syrup | 20 ml/4 tsp |
| 7.5 ml/1½ tsp | brandy | 15 ml/1 tbsp |
| 60 ml/4 tbsp | double cream whipped | 120 ml/8 tbsp |
| | cream and chocolate caraque, leaves or curls, to decorate (*optional*) | |

## One

1. Break the chocolate into a medium bowl and add the golden syrup and brandy. Microwave on MEDIUM for 2½-3 minutes, stirring twice until smooth. Allow to cool slightly.

2. Whip the cream until it stands in soft peaks, then fold into the chocolate mixture. Spoon into a dessert glass, level the surface and chill for about 2-4 hours.

3. Serve chilled. For a special touch top with a swirl of cream and decorate with chocolate caraque, leaves or curls.

## Two

1. Break the chocolate into a medium bowl and add the golden syrup and brandy. Microwave on MEDIUM for 3-3½ minutes, stirring twice until smooth. Allow to cool slightly.

2. Whip the cream until it stands in soft peaks, then fold into the chocolate mixture. Spoon into two dessert glasses, level the surface and chill for about 2-4 hours.

3. Serve chilled. For a special touch top each glass with a swirl of cream and decorate with chocolate caraque, leaves or curls.

# *Teacup Syllabub Trifles*

A few years ago, I inherited a number of very pretty, if non-matching teacups from my mother-in-law. We rarely take tea in the traditional fashion so they quickly gathered dust at the back of a cupboard. Until today that is, when I think they make the perfect container for a trifle for one or two - and they don't have to match!

| One | | Two |
|---|---|---|
| 75 g/3 oz | blackberries, tayberries or loganberries or a mixture of all three | 175 g/6 oz |
| 15 g/½ oz | sugar | 25 g/1 oz |
| 5 ml/1 tsp | water | 10 ml/2 tsp |
| 1 | trifle sponges | 2 |
| 15 g/½ oz | ratafias | 25 g/1 oz |
| 30 ml/2 tbsp | white wine | 60 ml/4 tbsp |
| 10 ml/2 tsp | lemon juice | 20 ml/4 tsp |
| 40 g/1½ oz | caster sugar | 75 g/3 oz |
| 75 ml/5 tbsp | double cream | 150 ml/¼ pt |
| ½ | egg white | 1 |
| | chopped toasted nuts, to decorate | |

## One

1. Place the berries in a small bowl with the sugar and water, cover and microwave on HIGH for 1 minute or until the juices run. Allow to cool.

2. Split the sponge cake and arrange over the base of a large deep teacup or an individual glass serving dish. Spoon the berries and their juice over the top. Cover in turn with the ratafias and chill thoroughly.

3. Pour the wine into a medium bowl and add the lemon juice and almost all of the sugar with the cream. Whisk until the mixture is thick and fluffy.

4. In a separate bowl, whisk the egg white until it stands in stiff peaks. Sprinkle over the remaining sugar and whisk until thick and glossy. Fold into the cream mixture with a metal spoon.

5. Spoon on top of the ratafias and chill for several hours before serving, sprinkled with toasted chopped nuts.

## Two

1. Place the berries in a small bowl with the sugar and water, cover and microwave on HIGH for 1½ minutes or until the juices run. Allow to cool.

2. Split the sponge cakes and arrange over the base of two large, deep teacups or two individual glass serving dishes. Spoon the berries and their juice equally over the top. Cover in turn equally with the ratafias and chill thoroughly.

3. Pour the wine into a medium bowl and add the lemon juice and almost all of the sugar with the cream. Whisk until the mixture is thick and fluffy.

4. In a separate bowl, whisk the egg white until it stands in stiff peaks. Sprinkle over the remaining sugar and whisk until thick and glossy. Fold into the cream mixture with a metal spoon.

5. Spoon equally over the top of the ratafias and chill for several hours before serving, sprinkled with toasted chopped nuts.

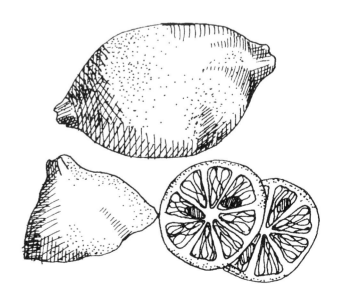

# American Apple 'Fall' Short Cakes

This is a speedy shortcake dessert recipe that can also be made with strawberries. Sprinkling the shortcake with a few chopped toasted nuts or toasted coconut helps to compensate for the lack of browning.

| One | | Two |
|---|---|---|
| 25 g/1 oz | plain flour | 50 g/2 oz |
| 2-2.5 ml/½ tsp | baking powder | 3.75 ml/¾ tsp |
| 20 g/¾ oz | butter or margarine | 40 g/1½ oz |
| 15 g/½ oz | caster sugar | 20 g/¾ oz |
| 5-7.5 ml/1-1½ tsp | milk | 10-15 ml/2-3 tsp |
| 5 ml/1 tsp | chopped toasted nuts or toasted coconut | 10 ml/2 tsp |
| | **Filling:** | |
| 1 | dessert apples, peeled, cored and sliced | 2 |
| | dash of lemon juice | |
| | pinch of ground cinnamon | |
| | dash of water | |
| 5-10 ml/1-2 tsp | apricot jam | 10-15 ml/2-3 tsp |
| 50 ml/2 fl oz | double cream, whipped | 125 ml/4 fl oz |
| 5-10 ml/1-2 tsp | sifted icing sugar | 10-15 ml/2-3 tsp |

## One

1. Sift the flour and the baking powder into a bowl, rub in the butter or margarine until the mixture resembles fine breadcrumbs, then stir in the sugar. Add just enough milk to bind the dough to a soft manageable consistency. Knead lightly on a floured surface and roll or flatten into a small round. Place on a greased cooking plate and sprinkle with the chopped nuts or coconut. Microwave on HIGH for 1-2 minutes, turning or rearranging once after 45 seconds, until well risen and cooked. Transfer to a wire rack to cool for 5 minutes, then split in half while still warm.

2. Meanwhile, place the apple in a small bowl with the lemon juice, cinnamon and barely enough water to moisten. Cover and microwave on HIGH for about 30 seconds or until the apple slices are just tender but not fallen. Drain thoroughly and toss gently in the apricot jam to coat lightly. Allow to cool.

3. Spread the bottom half of the shortcake with half of the whipped cream, then cover with the apple slices. Cover with the shortcake top and sprinkle with icing sugar. Pipe or spoon the remaining cream on top of the shortcake or on to a serving plate at the side of the finished shortcake. Serve on the day of making.

## Two

1. Sift the flour and baking powder into a bowl, rub in the butter or margarine until the mixture resembles fine breadcrumbs, then stir in the sugar. Add just enough milk to bind to a soft manageable consistency. Knead lightly on a floured surface, divide into two pieces and roll or flatten each piece into a small round. Place on a large greased baking plate so that they do not touch and are unlikely to do so when they rise and cook. Sprinkle with the chopped nuts or coconut. Microwave on HIGH for 2-3 minutes, turning or rearranging once after 1-1¼ minutes, until well risen and cooked. Transfer to a wire rack to cool for 5 minutes, then split each shortcake in half while still warm.

2. Meanwhile, place the apple in a medium bowl with the lemon juice, cinnamon and barely enough water to moisten. Cover and microwave on HIGH for about 1 minute or until the apple slices are just tender but not fallen. Drain thoroughly and toss gently in the apricot jam to coat lightly. Allow to cool.

3. Spread the bottom half of the shortcakes with half of the whipped cream, then cover equally with the apple slices. Cover with the shortcake tops and sprinkle with the icing sugar. Pipe or spoon the remaining cream on top of the shortcakes or on to two serving plates at the sides of the finished shortcakes. Serve on the day of making.

# Summer Berry Brûlées

These sensationally creamy brûlées can, of course, be served in the winter time, especially if you change the fruit accompaniment to winter exotic fruits like mango, pineapple and clementines. In the late summer, I love to serve them with tiny clusters of seedless grapes.

| One | | Two |
|---|---|---|
| 1 | egg yolks | 2 |
| 7 g/¼ oz | caster sugar | 15 g/½ oz |
| 150 ml/¼ pt | double cream | 300 ml/½ pt |
| 15 ml/1 tbsp | demerara sugar | 30 ml/2 tbsp |
| | **selection of summer fruit berries to serve (fraises du bois, raspberries, blueberries and cherries for example)** | |

## One

1. Whisk the egg yolk with the caster sugar and 10 ml/2 tsp of the cream. Place the remaining cream in a jug and microwave on HIGH for 20 seconds. Stir into the egg mixture, mixing well. Microwave on MEDIUM for 2-3 minutes, stirring 4 times, until the mixture is smooth and thickened and will coat the back of a wooden spoon.

2. Pour into a small ramekin dish or small heatproof dish and chill for at least 3-4 hours until set.

3. Sprinkle the top of the dish with the sugar to coat evenly, then cook under a preheated very hot grill for 1-2 minutes until the sugar caramelises. Allow to cool, then chill for a further 1-2 hours.

4. To serve, place the ramekin on an individual serving plate. Prepare the fruit according to type and use to surround the crème brûlée. Serve on the day of making.

## Two

1. Whisk the egg yolks with the caster sugar and 20 ml/4 tsp of the cream. Place the remaining cream in a jug and microwave on HIGH for 45 seconds. Stir into the egg mixture, mixing well. Microwave on MEDIUM for 4-6 minutes, stirring 4 times, until the mixture is smooth and thickened and will coat the back of a wooden spoon.

2. Pour into two small ramekin dishes or small heatproof dishes and chill for at least 3-4 hours until set.

3. Sprinkle the tops of the dishes evenly with the sugar to coat, then cook under a preheated very hot grill for 1-2 minutes until the sugar caramelises. Allow to cool, then chill for a further 1-2 hours.

4. To serve, place the ramekins on two individual serving plates. Prepare the fruit according to type and use to surround the crème brûlées. Serve on the day of making.